finishing

completing the race set before you

AS INTRODUCED IN THE BOOK *STUCK!*

TERRY B. WALLING
w/ Robert Grant

contents

Before Words	6
Dedications	10
Overview of *Finishing*	11

PART ONE: THE PURPOSE

1 IN-BETWEEN—The What	19
2 COUNTER-CULTURE—The How	27
3 CONVERGENCE—The Why	39

PART TWO: THE BRIDGE

4 STEPPING BACK—Phase One: Entry	51
Robert's Reflection	57
5 REARVIEW MIRROR—Phase Two: Evaluation	59
Robert's Reflection	64
6 A TIMELY WORD—Phase Three: Alignment	67
Robert's Reflection	73
7 DIFFERENT—Phase Four: Direction	75
Robert's Reflection	80
8 RESOLVE	83

PART THREE: THE APPLICATIONS

9 MEN & WOMEN	93
10 MINISTRY, MARKETPLACE & THE HOME	101
11 FINISHING: Pre-Retirement	109
12 FINISHING: Post-Retirement	115

PART FOUR: THE HELPS

13 FOUR POSTURES	123

14 THREE CONSTRUCTS	131
Five Words Exercise	132
Five Circles Exercise	133
Thirteen Ways—Concentric Circles Exercise	134
15 THE VALUE OF COACHING	139
The Resonance Online Process	140
The IDEA Coaching Pathway	142

NOTES 146

APPENDIX
A. Small Group Guide	149
B. Coaching Guide	160
C. Closure Paper Template	165
D. Leader Breakthru's Development Pathway	167

before words: *Terry*

I am in the end-game, but I am far from finished. I am on the path to finishing.
I could be at the same point in life as you.

I am 66 at the writing of this book.

At age 56, God called me and my wife to launch the Leader Breakthru ministry.

At age 45, I served as Vice President of a mission agency in the U.S.

At age 38, my wife Robin and I left the pastorate and joined a mission agency and moved to Australia for five years.

At age 28, I married Robin, and became Senior Pastor of the local church I had grown up in.

At age 18, I left home and attended a Christian college to play baseball, and to get a college education with a focus on Business Administration.

At age 16, I was named Teen Commissioner of my home town's Recreation and Parks Commission—only the second teenager in the U.S. to hold such a position.

At age 13, my parents, my sister and I were part of a church plant. It was a unique church, situated in a shopping center proclaiming that the church should be on mission. It was a church ahead of its time.

At age 7, my Dad landed a job in California as an aerospace engineer and participated in the U.S. Space program which was focused on putting a man on the moon. They did it.

At age 4, my family moved from Louisville, Kentucky to Hartford, Connecticut so my Dad could go to engineering school. The adventure for my folks began.

On October 15, 1952, I was born in Louisville, Kentucky.

Seen in reverse, I see more clearly how God has been at work shaping me. I now recognize the many deposits and entrustments that were placed into my life through the people, events and circumstances I encountered. Some things in my life have gone well, other moments have led to failure. Each moment has occurred with purpose. Some I understand, some I have yet to understand, and some I will never understand this side of heaven. Yet, I live under the banner of the Apostle Paul's declaration that: "all things work together for the good of those who love God, called according to His purpose (Romans 8:28).

This current season brings with it a unique set of questions, but one thing is certain—those who enter this time are not done. This next stage of development could prove to be the most important of our lives—yielding some of our most important Kingdom contributions. The Finishing Transition catapults Christ-followers into the third chapter of the journey with Christ and into a time of Convergence.

The concepts ahead are focused on helping people like you and me to finish well and to hear the words: "well done thou good and faithful servant."

Here's hoping you will.

Terry Walling
2019

before words: *Robert*

Early childhood memories of what I should expect from life involved working hard, being successful and then retiring! Otto Von Bismark decided on age 65 for retirement in 1880 because hardly anyone in Germany at that time lived to be 65! For various reasons, the idea stuck and was carried into the 20th century as a normal anticipation for the closing years of life. That's what I was taught.

But when I turned 65, I knew I was not done. I am 77 at this writing.

The cultural mandate said: "Leave the playing field, go to the bench, pack your things and leave the stadium. You are done. You've had a successful career, now go play, you deserve it. Go away." Associates looked past me to younger leaders to fill roles I knew I was better equipped to fill.

My years of education, experience and giftedness had converged and pointed to the potential of my most significant contribution. These moments yielded some of the most difficult twists and turns of my life. I had to face the reality that too much of my identity was tied to my work and performance. An internal war raged on between the cultural norm of "retiring" and my sense that my best service to others was yet to come.

My Finishing Transition proved to be the unique moment when God deepened my convictions about His call upon my life and told me that I was not done until He said I was "done." Being coached during this defining moment was key to discovering God's designs and purposes for life beyond the cultural expectations, and it showed me how life could look beyond my own self-imposed limitations.

Terry Walling coached me through this time of swimming upstream. His patient inquiry helped me gain new clarity about the future and the rich deposits that had been made by the Spirit during my life and its many crucible moments. I needed an alongside guide and a voice who could engage me where I was, and help me become clear about what God was doing. The coaching helped me sort myself out on both a head and heart level. Terry was the right person at the right time with the right gifts that gave me a quiet confidence and direction for the important steps I needed to take into my future.

In *Finishing*, I try to offer you a candid picture of my own journey with both the hopes and questions that you may encounter should you find yourself in a similar place. Sometimes seeing where you are by considering another person's story can alert you to the value and God's forming work in your own circumstances.

Be encouraged. Know that others have been where you are, and were able to experience a new sense of purpose. I hope that hearing of my story and its challenges can become a broken bread shared for nourishment of those who find themselves in the Finishing Transition. My prayerful desire is that some of what is shared here will contribute to a breakthrough in your own personal journey. If that can occur, that will yield the warmth of my smile.

Robert Grant
2019

thanks & dedications

Thanks to the leaders who have gone before me and showed it was possible to finish well.

In particular I dedicate this to my mentor, Dr. J. Robert "Bobby" Clinton. For all I learned from his teaching, but also for how he lived his message, and for how he passed on what God had given him to many like me.

—Terry Walling

To every pilgrim willing to step into uncharted territory to create a path for others and to my wife, Sue, who has joined her faith with mine for 55 years of loving support as I have pursued the upward call.

—Robert Grant

overview of *finishing*

WHO IS *FINISHING* WRITTEN FOR?

Finishing has been written for those whose bucket list is far from complete. It has been written for those focused on what they will lay before the feet of their King when they arrive home. They seek to have their life resound beyond their years.

They are finishing. But they are not finished.

The word "retirement" is not in their vocabulary.

Finishers do not want to retreat from their engagement in or contribution to society. They are eager to develop new focused activity, daily rhythms, habits of conduct, and vehicles for delivering meaning and help to others. Finishers still yearn for lives of purposefulness and continued learning.[1]

This book has two audiences, each committed to finishing well.

1. Pre-retirement—Those in their 60s who are wondering what life will look like when they step away from active, full-time employment, and how they will handle the changes ahead. Will they still have a work to do?

2. Experiencing retirement—Those who have crossed over the cultural threshold of 66+ and are often busier than they were before they retired, and wondering what happened. They are seeking clarity and ways to sort out the many needs and opportunities they now confront. What is the work God still has for them to do?

Both groups find themselves in the midst of a time of transition. They know they cannot go back to how they used to live, but they are not sure how to navigate the days ahead. The question for both is not "why?" but "how?"

The Finishing Transition occurs for those in their 60s and 70s. It serves to catalyze the third and most important stage of one's life and work. In our early years we discover the work God has for each of us to do. In the middle years we seek to do that work, whether at home, in the marketplace or in vocational ministry. In the third and final strategic segment of life, time-tested Christ-followers find themselves navigating questions of ultimate contribution and the cultural illusion of "retirement." Ahead of these Christ-followers is a series of choices that will mold their life and lifestyle in their final days. It is a call to finish well.

Sarah Lawerence-Lightfoot in her book, *The Third Chapter* states, "This transition—sometimes abrupt and at other times protracted—is usually a time of fear, ambivalence, and chaos, during which it is hard to articulate where you are heading, or how you will get there, and life feels out of balance and unfocused." This transition instigates change and consolidation.

Ralph Nader, activist of the 70s made the observation that, "A generational stirring is rumbling among those who grew up in the 50s and 60s when America was number one in just about everything and who now find their land in deep trouble on almost all fronts. With their children raised and some financial security achieved, more of them are looking outward to help solve the country's problems."[2]

The desire of Christ for each of our lives remains clear, "I have come that they may have life, and have it to the full" (John 10:10). Life to the fullest has little to do with stage of life, possessions, or title. God's sovereign deposits into our lives are designed to be entrusted to others.

Getting the Most out of *Finishing*

This book is sourced in the forty years of lifelong, personal development research from Dr. J. Robert Clinton, a former Professor at Fuller Seminary and author of *The Making of a Leader* and in the thirty-plus years of personal development coaching by myself (Dr. Terry Walling), the President of Leader Breakthru. I first authored the book *Stuck! Navigating the Transitions of Life & Leadership* which introduces the Finishing Transition. This book seeks to provide a more full definition of that transition.

Leadership Emergence Patterns, researched and developed by Dr. Clinton, is the study of how God shapes the lives of His followers for influence over their lifetimes. Transition moments play a big part of that shaping work. Staying the course during a time of transition is no easy feat. Transitions often challenge a believer's trust, driving them into deeper times of intimacy with Christ, and are often more about perseverance than immediate insight.

Here are three ways to read *Finishing*, and how you can best use this book to help you run your race in the midst of this time of transition.

First, read *Finishing* as an overall interpretive guide.

Though your time of transition will feel unique and personal to you, use these concepts as a guide and map—helping to provide language, definition, labels and landmarks. Not everything that you are facing in your time of transition will be the same as what you read about, but the words contained often provide reassurance and hope. It helps to know that you are not alone in what you are experiencing. The more common the path the better the ability to navigate this new landscape.

Second, utilize *Finishing* as an interactive tool designed to be read and explored with others.

We do not get to clarity alone. Walking with others through these insights helps give us courage to not abandon the work God is doing. Many who have benefited from the concepts within have done so with the help of a friend, a coach or a small group who are encountering the same challenges. Going together, in the context of community, helps you get all you can out of this moment. There are coaching questions and a small group guide in the Appendices to help you.

Third, allow *Finishing* to be a compass as you seek to chart the days ahead.

Don't rush through this time. Allow God time and space to work. Transitions can take time—from three months to three years. Sometimes you will need to come back to this information and process issues more fully. Similar to how Abraham was told to pack up and leave with no announced destination, God is taking you to a new place, and it may take a while to get there. Some of these insights will make sense right away and some will require time. Let as many impending decisions, as possible, be held loosely until you have gained both the insight and assurance that you have heard God's shepherding voice.

Every attempt to go to a new place can be benefited by the help of a guide. Your navigational guides through the Finishing Transition are myself and Robert Grant.

I (Terry) coach, resource and provide training in the area of personal development and coaching. I am passionate to come alongside and walk with risk-taking, Kingdom leaders. I will be your main guide through the Finishing Transition as I coach a fellow traveler like yourself (Robert Grant) through the often disappearing path of the Finishing Transition.

Robert Grant is a coach, Christian leader and one who pastors other leaders. Though it will be his Finishing Transition we will work our way through, Robert too will serve as a guide as he offers you a look inside his transition and his very real issues and challenges. The narrative of Robert's transition has been adapted to fit the format of the book but it references how the Finishing Transition typically progresses. Robert shares his honest reactions to the transition, as it occurred, in the narrative sections and through his journal entries.

After the release of my book *Stuck!*, individuals voiced a desire for greater help with each of the three transitions introduced in the book—Awakening, Deciding and Finishing. Three books have now been written, one on each of the three transitions. *Finishing* is the third and final book in this series on life transitions. Each book is detailed on the Leader Breakthru website (leaderbreakthru.com) and can be purchased online.

***Finishing* is organized into four-parts:**

Part One provides a concise, clear description of transitions, and specifically the Finishing Transition. Characteristics, core components, and critical issues of the Finishing Transition will be explored. Chapter 1 focuses on "the what" of the transition, Chapter 2 focuses on "the how" and Chapter 3 focuses on "the why." Together, they give an overview and some initial help for moving into this third chapter of our lives in Christ.

Part Two chronicles the actual Finishing Transition of Robert Grant. Together, Robert and I share a summarized version of the coaching conversations that actually took place. His story is real and the issues that are discussed are the actual ones we worked through. Robert also shares his personal thoughts and feelings as he processed the raw emotions that surfaced as a result of experiencing this in-between moment.

Part Three provides interpretive helps. Chapter 9 speaks to how the feeling of being set-aside or passed over is often the set-up for Convergence. Chapter 10 speaks to the different ways that men and women experience the Finishing Transition. Chapter 11 looks at the contextual factors that those in the marketplace and vocational ministry feel as they work through issues. And Chapter 12 goes deeper in processing the unique challenges of this transition for people in both pre- and post-retirement.

Part Four offers exercises and resources to help you process the Finishing Transition. Chapter 13 unpacks three exercises that help identify what a Christ-follower has to offer in the end-game. Chapter 14 highlights different ways that those who have finished well contribute to others in the end game. Chapter 15 introduces you to the *Resonance Online Process* from Leader Breakthru and how it can help bring clarity and insights.

PART ONE

the purpose

Isn't it funny how day by day nothing changes, but when you look back everything is different.[3]

—C.S. LEWIS

He is no fool who gives what he cannot keep, to gain what he cannot lose.[4]

—JIM ELLIOT

WHAT'S AHEAD?

The first chapters of *Finishing* focus on God's purposes during the third and most important transition of a Christ-follower's discipleship. The Finishing Transition ushers in a time of Convergence and the discovery of one's ultimate contribution. This strategic transition occurs somewhere in the early 60s to mid 70s.

Chapters 1-3 offer key characteristics and insights related to aligning your current experiences with how God is shaping your future work and influence as a committed Christ-follower. Chapter 1 specifically seeks to offer descriptions and definition related to the Finishing Transition. These topics will be unpacked throughout the book, but we offer you some key insights up front to help you gain your bearings. Transitions are unique, defining moments in the lives of all Christ-followers. They can also be destabilizing.

The issues addressed in these next chapters include:

- Defining transitions and specifically the nature of the Finishing Transition
- Norming the emotions related to what might be occurring
- Helping align your current experience with how transitions occur
- Identifying what's critical to navigating the Finishing Transition
- Describing the end-game and the experience of Convergence

1

in-between

THE WHAT

The terrible thing, the almost impossible thing, is to hand over your whole self—all your wishes and precautions—to Christ.[5]

—C.S. LEWIS

Do not look for shortcuts to God. The market is flooded with surefire, easygoing formulas for successful life that can be practiced in your spare time. Do not fall for that stuff, even though crowds of people do. The way of life—to God —is vigorous and requires total attention.

—MATTHEW 7:13-14 (THE MESSAGE)

Transitions are like eddies that occur within the flow of a river. Eddies form off to the side, often unnoticed, and are powerful in their flow. They are spotted because of the funnel-type flow of the water—a whirlpool that spins and disrupts the current, sweeping up anything in its path into its ongoing circular motion. Eddies often occur behind a boulder wedged into the onrush of a river, near a tree log that seems to be blocking the flow of the water, or in a deep-pool that hides under the depth of the riverbed. The swirling motion is sometimes more turbulent and stronger than the rest of the current. A piece of driftwood can get caught in that flow and circle for hours as it churns around and around, over and over again. Over time the mass of material eventually works its way to the outer rims of the swirl, and then is released from the control of the circular current and makes its way back out and into the mainstream of the river. On it goes.

All believers face these "off to the side" moments throughout their journey. Some of these turning points are more strategic than others. The Finishing Transition is a strategic turning point in the life of a Christ-follower that moves them from where they are now, into a time of finishing well. God does some of His most important work during these in-between, transition moments—depositing insights and values that serve to guide one's life and ministry. You have been here before.

The Awakening Transition occurs in the 20s-30s and focuses on issues of clarifying Calling. The Deciding Transition occurs in the 40s-50s and seeks to define issues of Contribution. The Finishing Transition occurs in the 60s-70s and moves a Christ-follower into a time of Convergence. All transitions share some common characteristics, regardless of when they occur. They are often signaled by times of:

- Restlessness
- Prolonged confusion
- New or re-surfacing self-doubt
- Lack of motivation
- Prolonged inactivity or paralysis
- Continuing uncertainty

- Diminished confidence
- Continued lack of clarity

There are unique characteristics that occur during the Finishing Transition, including:

- Questions related to retirement and what is next
- Uncertainty related to living without position
- Questions related to one's purpose, focus and meaningful activity
- Struggles with being set-aside or placed "on the bench"
- Problems with deciding on where to focus efforts
- Challenges related to financial security vs. Kingdom focus
- Sustained questions related to what one has to offer others

Regardless of the transition, one thing is common: **if you find yourself in a time of transition, help is needed now**. Transitions net confusion and uncertainty. Gaining a better handle on what is occurring and some understanding of what God could be at work doing is essential. This chapter seeks to do just that.

The next pages offer concise descriptors related to the Finishing Transition and what it entails. The topics and issues within this chapter will be unpacked throughout this book, but we offer you some key insights up front.

Typical age/duration of the Finishing Transition

Often occurs in one's early 60s to mid 70s and is wrapped around the issue of retirement, and what is next. The transition can occur over months or years.

Purpose of the Finishing Transition:

Consolidation of one's life experience and shaping related to doing less and having greater impact, finishing well and leaving behind a godly legacy.

Importance of the Finishing Transition:

Adopting a stewardship mentality, discovering and entrusting one's insights and counteracting the "retirement" (rest) mentality found within the culture.

What's at stake?

Will you finish well and hear the words of *"well done"* (Matthew 25)? Will you finish this life more in love with Christ, more passionate about His mission, and more sacrificial of your time, talent and treasure at the end, than you were at the beginning?

What occurs?

A series of paradigm shifts that move an individual into an influence orientation as opposed to a positional/vocational orientation. Spiritual authority offers greater potential for influence at this stage of life.

What helps to move the Finishing Transition forward?

A commitment to change, focus and greater intentionality in the days ahead, along with a willingness to make one's life more accessible to others by adopting a relational-empowerment approach to life and ministry.

What works against this time of transition?

Adopting an entitlement mindset. Thinking that contribution is now for the young or that you have nothing to offer.

How can others help?

Allow others to travel alongside you to offer coaching and encouragement. We do not get to clarity alone. Others can help you process your past journey and what you offer to others, and they can offer accountability as you navigate the change.

What are some of the emotions that often accompany the Finishing Transition?

- Excitement yet apprehension
- Passion to finish well and make a difference

- Frustration and even anger related to being benched or set aside
- Resolve to see the end-game done well
- Uncertainty, questions and fear about how the next chapter will work
- Seeking adventure—wanting to step into new opportunities and experiences
- Confusion and lack of focus
- Wonder about how life works when the job or position goes away
- Sorting of options related to what to do, where to go, and what's important
- Mixture of fun and fear—wanting to be free but not knowing what that means
- Pondering related to what to offer to others
- Unsure about what God wants/expects for this phase of the journey

The Finishing Transition Facts

- Transitions take time (from 3 months to 3 years)
- God does some of His greatest work during transition periods
- Get all you can out of a transition—quit fighting God and join Him
- Most need the help of another (a coach) to process how God is working
- Values are often clarified, convictions are often deepened
- God is doing a deeper work in order to do a greater work
- We are shaped, developed and discipled over our entire lifetime
- There is no such thing as retirement
- It is possible to have influence without position
- Legacy is a by-product and a result of choosing to live a life that resounds beyond your days.

HOW TRANSITIONS OCCUR

Transitions often follow a similar pattern.

The *Transition Life Cycle* (below) reveals the potential pathway and progression for your Finishing Transition. Each of the four segments of a transition comprises people, events and circumstances that keep moving a Christ-follower toward the next chapter in their development, even in the midst of living in the in-between.

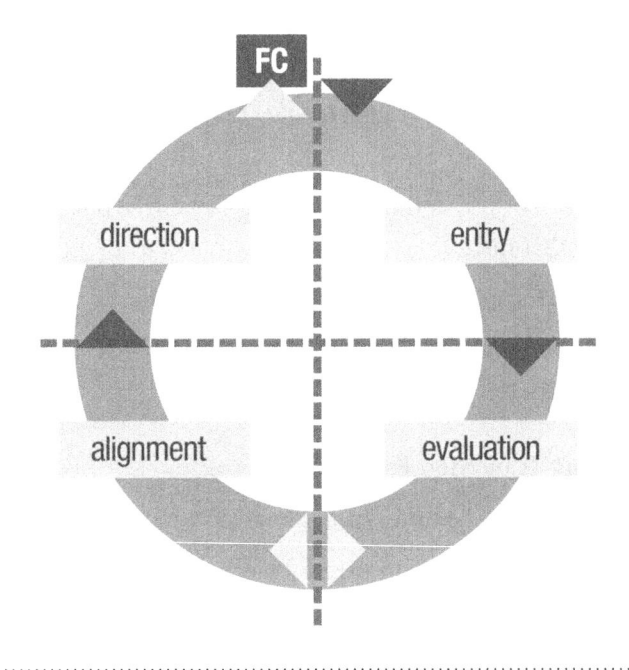

The Transition Life Cycle

The four segments of a transition are:

ENTRY: Initial days when you typically try many ways to solve the issues you are facing until you realize that something different is occurring.

EVALUATION: Seeking God and determining what is occurring and why. God at first might be silent, then He begins to reveal issues of healing, closure and new insights.

ALIGNMENT: Surrendering to God and His work, allowing Him to do a deeper work and move us closer in intimacy and trust. God gives first insights related to the purpose of the transition, and what could be ahead.

- Much of a transition is spent moving back-and-forth between Evaluation and Alignment.
- Most people in a transition experience times of quietness from God and are challenged to adopt new rhythms and practices to better hear and recognize His voice.

DIRECTION: Unfolding of the way forward, often involving a series of events and ending with a Faith Challenge as God calls you to step out and trust Him as He leads you into the future.

THE POINT?

Something different has begun.

Like the transitions that proceeded it, the Finishing Transition is a core tool that God uses to shape a Christ-follower. It surfaces new questions and new paradigms needed for the end-game. Though many questions will remain unanswered at this point, God is not done shaping each of our lives for Kingdom influence. What you and I have to offer, and God's designs for our future, far surpass words like "retirement," "empty-nest" and "a life of leisure." Words like these are being spoken all around us, but for passionate believers, they are shoes that do not fit. The desire placed within each of our hearts to contribute has been placed there by our God. Though each of us may not see a clear path forward at this point, direction is coming.

Before continuing, spend a few moments reflecting on your current experience in light of the summary of the Finishing Transition. Reflect on these questions and journal your thoughts.

1. What factors are present in your current experience?
2. What insights do you have related to how God might be at work?
3. What resistance do you feel in even considering these issues?

finishing

WANT MORE?

Here is a link to Leader Breakthru's website that will take you further on topics covered in this chapter:

www.leaderbreakthru.com/stuck-the-book

2

counter-culture

THE HOW

And what if Christ's call in our lives is not to conform to our culture? What if Christ in us compels us to counter our culture?[6]

—DAVID PLATT

Our business is to present the Christian faith clothed in modern terms, not to propagate modern thought clothed in Christian terms. Confusion here is fatal.[7]

—J.I. PACKER

SNAPSHOTS OF FINISHERS

He is 59 years old…

He was considering the biggest decision of his life—to sell his dental practice. For the last few years he has known that there was something more, beyond just continuing to grow his practice. He wanted to take his vocational skills to countries that needed them the most, and have his dentistry skills provide him an entry into places and experiences that could better allow him to live out his faith. His faith has been worked out in the suburbs he has inhabited most of his life, but would it work around the world? Would his faith be the same as when he was helping construct a sound foundation to young men and emerging Christ-followers? He was beginning to realize that his greatest moments in life had not been tooth abstractions, but rather, times when his income base and his unique skills had provided him time to listen, coach and mentor the hungry, the hurting, and especially the emerging leaders who faced questions related to faith and God's faithfulness. He was not quite sure how this would all work out, but the more he moved toward this moment, the more he knew it was something God wanted him to do! Something inside him was saying, "its time." And though he still felt he had many years to contribute, he knew this decision set up his most important days. Is he retiring? Hardly!

She's 63 years young …

She is gifted to nurture and care for others. Almost every thought within her is about solving problems and finding ways to better care for those she loves and desires to help. Everyone sees this about her, and even seeks to help her by acknowledging her gifting. Her contribution has now surfaced in new expressions beyond her most important work as a mother and a grandmother. She will always first care for family, but as her family grows, the empty nest season has launched something new. Her experience in the home has readied her to care for others in need. Her ability to solve problems and care for details could be applied to those within the organization she finds herself working in. She now serves the needs of those who desire to finish well. She has never been a fan of titles or labels, but, ironically, she now finds herself as the "administrator" of a Christian ministry. She troubleshoots and seeks to help others receive the help and resources they need. She feels that she is just being herself, but others see that what she offers is invaluable. Her greatest act of worship is offering all of who she is to those she serves—helping her family and others better advance Christ's Kingdom. Who she is matches what she does—allowing her to move into a time of life convergence.

He really can't believe it, but he is 71 years old…

He still feels strong and ready to take on ministry, but he realizes it is time to pass the reins onto a younger, even more gifted leader than himself. He has had a good run. He planted the church and had the opportunity to be there long-term. He has seen many families come through, and now the kids are leaders in the church. He is excited for what is next. He knows that he has made a difference. But now he is excited to do some teaching, to offer encouragement to some of the younger pastors in the area, and to coach some leaders who serve in the marketplace. They want his help figuring out how their business can make a Kingdom difference. And oh yeah, he wants to make time to be with his kids and grandkids. He took some time off, away from the church, to give the new Vicar time to settle in. It's his church to lead now. His new role is to be accessible to those God has already brought down his path, as well as to those who he has yet to recognize.

She's 73 years old and still going strong…

She used to be a nurse, and now, at heart, she remains someone who wants people to thrive and grow. Professionally she wandered into education administration and ended up serving many higher learning institutions. She migrated all the way up to President of several colleges. She has lived a busy and productive life. After stepping aside, she chose to serve on the board of a Christian college, and was thrust into the role of interim-chair of the board as it faced a traumatic moment in its history—one that threatened its survival. Her skills and integrity came together. She was trusted because of her gifting and because of her experience. A hard truth was faced. Tough decisions were made. Storms came and went. She was used by the Lord to lead them to the other side. The board ended up honoring her service by naming their School of Nursing after her. She was not seeking recognition. Awards had already been afforded to her. She just wanted to make a difference, and she saw a task that must be done.

I (Terry) am often asked, "what will life look like as I enter the Finishing Transition and this third chapter of life?" It looks like the men and women described above as they transition into a time of ultimate contribution. They are not finished, but they have chosen to lean into this time of transition and make the choices necessary to live into all of whom God has shaped them to be. They are neither young nor old. They are very much alive and they are passionate to finish well.

- We see it in the dentist who has entered the pre-retirement age and decides to sell his dental practice to help insure that his finish makes a difference. He represents Christ-followers who are coming up on Convergence, and illustrates how God can use one's restlessness and hunger to set up this next major stage in one's development. The selling of the business is not Convergence, but the process is being used by God to help him discover how He desires to use his life in the days ahead. The dentist's spiritual gifts, passion for the poor and dentistry skills are all beginning to converge together to reveal a purpose and contribution still very much in formation.

- We see it in a mother who is moving into new opportunities even as she continues to struggle to recognize her skills, experiences and contribution. She represents many who often discount and minimize their value and ability to work outside their previous contexts. Her gifting and abilities have been in formation all of her life, and are now being brought together to be expressed in new ways she had previously thought impossible.

- It looks like the pastor, who represents those in vocational ministry, who can often become too defined by their job, position or role. This pastor has chosen to not see himself only through that lens. The loss of position does not mean the loss of influence, especially in light of the spiritual authority God has given

- him in the lives of many. Defining his new role around how he can help, as opposed to the position he holds, is key as he chooses to stay in the game.

- We see it also in the board member who used her abilities to help rescue a college that was in trouble, bringing to bear a wide-variety of experiences and just-in-time counsel. Her story represents the coming together of skills, abilities and character to do something one has been shaped to do, but not for the sake of an award, notoriety or acclaim, but because it needs to be done, and can be done using one's entrustments. The Kingdom's advance was possible because this board member stepped in.

The list could go on and on, and it does. Many individuals are passionate about finishing well and living life with a sovereign perspective—seeing the end-game as being divinely shaped by all the people, events and circumstances present throughout one's life. Erik Erikson, a German-born, American developmental psychologist coined the phrase, "identity crisis." Erickson believed that one's identity and influence emerges over time, and that it is vital for men and women to take a lifelong, developmental approach to understanding one's identity as a key to understanding one's unique role.[8]

Jimmy Carter, the 39th President of the United States, occupied a seat of influence as President that very few have known. At his disposal were resources, power and authority. He could order men into war, distribute resources for disasters and call leaders together to bring peace to a contentious world. Whatever your political views are of Carter and his time as President, one thing stands out about his life that is glaringly obvious—he exhibited an even greater influence *after* leaving the office of the Presidency. His post-presidential humanitarian efforts and negotiation with world leaders exceeds his accomplishments while holding the office of President.

Position is not the best predictor of influence, especially when it comes to those transitioning into the third chapter of their journey. Disciples are shaped over time for influence. Influence is tied to our response to God's shaping work, as opposed to position or title. Jimmy Carter is an example of a Christ-follower who continues to weave together his experiences, assignments, deep core values, and years of wisdom into a set of unique ways to influence others. The Finishing Transition challenges the notion that position or vocation is required to offer influence. Instead, it offers an alternative—a counter-cultural way that believes influence comes from one's life, and that position exists only to help deliver influence.

JESUS NEVER STOPS DISCIPLING HIS DISCIPLES. THERE IS NO SUCH THING AS "RETIREMENT."

While energies do lessen and financial resources tighten, this final stage of life was never intended by God to be a time of "burying" one's talents, life experiences and resources (Matthew 25: 14-30). The Christ-like life is always about stewardship—investing in and empowering others—whether we find ourselves at the beginning or the end of our journey.

Jesus called for life to be lived to its fullest: *"The thief comes only to steal and kill and destroy; I have come that they may have life, and have it to the full"* (John 10:10). We are called to run the race of life and not just to finish, but to win: *"Do you not know that in a race all the runners run, but only one gets the prize? Run in such a way as to get the prize"* (1 Corinthians 9:24). And God's design is for each of us to contribute good deeds which He authored before time began: *"For we are God's handiwork, created in Christ Jesus to do good works, which God prepared in advance for us to do"* (Ephesians 2:10). Together, these verses tell of Christ-followers who are passionate to finish well. They are lifelong learners who experience times of repeated renewal and deeper growth, and they hunger for the adventure that these final days offer.

There are Christ-followers who have taken a different path. They decide to protect their life in the end-game, rather than continue to live their life. They settle-in, plateau and arrest in their development, going back in time to when they felt the most alive, hoping they can just stay there. These also hold back the Church—locking up resources and restricting the younger generations from leading the Church forward.

What they fail to realize is that discipleship with Christ never stops. It continues to move and life is found in the living.

Passionate, God-worshipers choose to live their lives at the end far differently from those who have plateaued or from a culture that continues to plan and posture for "retirement." Joseph's most important days were his final days. Paul modeled a life that finished well and served to the end. Caleb was faithful and passionate at the end and was given the right with Joshua to enter that long-promised land. Mary treasured all the times with Christ, and stayed true even in the midst of struggle and challenge. John lived a life focused on a new heaven and earth. On and on goes the list. Hebrews 11 tells of those who lived their faith to the end.

We who love Christ live in an upside-down Kingdom. Though many in church often wander away from God's purposes and plans, there are still many who choose to live a life far different than what surrounds them. It is a life lived to its fullest even to the end, and a life that leaves behind a godly legacy.

Consider some additional thoughts related to this issue of "retirement." The speed of change permeates every aspect of our lives today. What once was the norm in terms of behavior and accepted approaches to life, has changed in our lifetime. Our current views of retirement and its varied behaviors grew out of the "New Deal" era and the 1935 Social Security Act. It was a time when American workers had the right to retire and a right to live without working, after age sixty-five.[9] These norms were written over eighty years ago and now project a shadow and image that many in America, including Christians, use to base their expectations for life after 65. We have come to believe that when the 60s arrive, we are often "too old to work, but too young to die." Yet, deep inside of us we know this is not the case. We actually hunger to contribute more.

The following statistics are not new, but they highlight the realities that now surround the issue of life after age 65, especially for those in the west, and for those believers who are facing the end-game and a time of Convergence:

- The large number of people within the Boomer generation is combined with a greater life expectancy than earlier generations.

- The next generation of Americans (after the Boomers) age sixty-plus is expected to be the healthiest and longest living in history.[10]
- The percentage of retirement age Americans who live until the age of ninety has almost doubled over the last forty years.[11]
- 60% of those between the ages of 55 and 74 plan to work during retirement.
  - 34% of those plan to work part-time within their interest areas.
  - 19% will work beyond 65 for additional income.
  - 10% of these plan to start their own businesses.[12]
- Up to 31% of all Baby Boomers graduated from college, whereas as low as 16.7% of older, previous generations did.[13]
- According to the U.S. Bureau of Labor Statistics, by 2020, one out of every four working Americans will be 55 and older.

These statistics and percentages vary based on geographic areas but the facts point to a new time—an end-game that is different for all of us who live and lead in today's ever-changing society. At a minimum, those who are in their 60s or 70s today will average another 10 to potentially 20 years of active mission and ministry, and most who are passionate Christ-followers long for greater Kingdom contribution. But to circle back and state the obvious again, the danger has come as the Church shrinks back from a life designed by God, and slips into a life lived according to the morays of the culture. God never stops discipling his disciples. Our role is to live life to its fullest as we allow God to grow this new life deeper into our lives.

CULTURAL NORMS

In order to counteract the norms that continue to be reinforced by our culture, we first must call them out and recognize their strong influence on the thought processes and conversations that surround our end-game strategies. Many people view these norms as "rites of passage" for those crossing over into retirement. They typically fall into one of the following three entitlements—or cultural norms.

The Norm of Rest

This is the growing desire to relinquish responsibilities, service and even engagement because of the tiredness that comes from years of active involvement. The conversation around the table moves to arguing that it's time for the young to assume responsibility for what needs to occur, and to begin to come to grips with the effort required. It's time for those who have served to finally rest—they have earned their break.

- **What's true:** Engagement and serving, over time takes its toll. Carrying responsibilities and demands gets old. And the older one gets, the more challenging and demanding the tasks get.

- **What's missed:** Rest can often produce loss of commitment or growth. Rest does not mean full relinquishment. It should refer more to adapting, changing or downsizing one's multiple roles and responsibilities to match the new realities of less energy and capacity.

- **What's lost:** When this norm is adopted, the adventure begins to end. The loss of involvement often means the loss of contact. And the chance to "rub shoulders" with others, especially the younger generation, is lost. It is in the task that values are revealed and relationships are forged.

Seek ye first the Kingdom of God, and his righteousness, and all these things will be added to you. (Matthew 6:33, KJV)

The Norm of Reward

This is the entitlement norm that believes after years of sacrificing for others, it is now time for us. While they have been serving, others have been enjoying. Now it's our turn. This norm moves into a time where lifestyle now includes leisure, consumption and justifying the expending of one's resources on personal wants and desires. The rationale is that it's now time for us to enjoy our lives. This norm sets up a dichotomy between one's life before and one's life now, as if they are two different lives.

- **What's true:** Many of life's demands and duties have often crowded out time to travel, or even enjoy much of the life that surrounds us. While few in the world have opportunities to think in these terms, nonetheless, ideas of travel and enjoyment are not outside the scope of the Kingdom life.

- **What's missed:** Reward and entitlement are dangerous measuring sticks. With so much need surrounding us, consuming for the value of consumption is not a Kingdom lifestyle. Utilizing our resources at the end differently, being freed up to help and minister to others is a Kingdom value. Travel, serving and moving into new opportunities can keep the adventure alive.

- **What's lost:** Entitlement is self-centeredness, pure and simple. To adopt a life posture of "I deserve" as opposed to "I have been given" works against the very nature of the gospel and the grace of Christ that has been shown to us. We each have been given much. Our job now is to give. Generosity and gratitude produce life. Entitlement seeks only to rob.

"For I was hungry and you gave me something to eat, I was thirsty and you gave me something to drink, I was a stranger and you invited me in, I needed clothes and you clothed me, I was sick and you looked after me, I was in prison and you came to visit me."
—Matthew 25:35-36

The Norm of Retreat

This is the desire to go off and just be by ourselves, whether in the mountain hideaway, the country-side home or some retirement village or less populated area—to finally have the nice, quiet life. This norm has appeals to many who have worked hard, who are tired of all the demands and pressures, and who would rather just "sit by the dock of the bay."

- **What's true:** As life goes longer, our lifestyles change. The appeal that came from the rush, the busyness and the challenges no longer attracts us. Time away, and even time in other venues often provide the rest and ability to soldier on. Life today is a life of noise. Solitude and time to live around new landscapes and environments is life-giving.

- **What's missed:** Retreat brings with it the potential of growing isolation. Often we hide instead of grow during times of retreat. Being away can heal, but it can often harm. It allows us to retreat back within ourselves, arresting our growth and development by sealing ourselves off from the world and interaction.

- **What's lost:** Spiritual formation comes as we interact both with our God, with our understanding of ourselves and with others. Community is key to formation. Though our lives may have been wounded and even scarred through the interactions of life, being engaged with others in day-to-day life is one of the core tools the Potter uses to shape our lives. The loss of others often means the loss of life.

It is time to re-think how many, even in the Church today, are approaching their finishing years.

John Piper—pastor, author and speaker—has challenged Christians in America to live counter-culturally with regards to retirement. Let his words sink in:

> "What a tragedy is occurring in America today.
>
> This is one of the biggest tragedies in our culture. That billions of dollars are invested every year to get people my age to waste the rest of their lives. This tragedy is called 'retirement.'
>
> While the world is uncared for medically, uneducated, drinking filthy water, are poverty ridden and un-evangelized, these needs sink under the weight of healthy 65 year old people playing bridge, shuffleboard and collecting shells, fishing and golfing their way into the presence of King Jesus. And you and I are going to join them my friends unless we make some very radical decisions and commitment about where your treasure is."[14]

THE POINT?

It is possible that you are tired—beat up by life and its challenges—and you want to rest and to cease striving. But ahead is something more. The Finishing Transition is a border crossing. It is the entrance to the third stage of one's discipleship as a Christ-follower. Life is not over. A significant chapter has yet to be lived. Ahead is a new place and a life of focus and intention. Those who have gone before us have discovered that life is in the finishing, and have learned how to finish well.

We close this chapter with a question:

> *If you knew God would give you another ten to twenty years of good health and energy to live, to help advance Christ's Kingdom and life to others, what would you do with those years?*

Convergence is when all of life begins to "resonate" together just like the instruments of an orchestra playing in perfect pitch and harmony, resulting in beautiful music that's never been heard before.

WANT MORE?

Here is a link to Leader Breakthru's website that will take you further on topics covered in this chapter:

lbu.leaderbreakthru.com/products/five-choices

3

convergence

THE WHY

*We never grow closer to God when we just live life.
It takes deliberate pursuit and attentiveness.* [15]

—FRANCIS CHAN

*He who lays up treasures on earth spends his life backing away from his treasures. To him, death is loss. He who lays up treasures in heaven looks forward to eternity; he's moving daily toward his treasures.
To him, death is gain.* [16]

—RANDY ALCORN

THE END OR THE BEGINNING?

I was not expecting to be on the bench.

Watching others play the game and get the nod to do what I had been shaped to contribute left me feeling overlooked, under appreciated and no longer needed. Using the sports analogy, I was use to being in the game, making the plays and actively being a part of the starting team. I had been quietly demoted from being an essential contributor, to just being a spectator. I was consumed with a restless fidgeting over not being on the field. It was a major change that rocked me in ways for which I was not prepared.

My first acquaintance with a "bench experience" came early. It came from sports. It happened in the sixth grade at John Tyler Elementary School in Portsmouth, Virginia. Team captains had been selected for a softball game during our daily gym period. Captains were picked, and they alternated selecting players for team positions. We each eagerly waited for our name to be called in hopes of getting our favorite spot on the field. When my name was called, I heard the word "bench" fill the air, like it had been yelled through a megaphone. It was punctuated by belly laughs from my classmates. It was humiliating. In an instant, "the bench" was seared in my journey by both the humiliation of my peers, and a place for the discards. It defined me in the eyes of my classmates and left me feeling isolated and not needed.

Eventually, I moved off the bench. I started demonstrating skills on the field, hitting a few home runs, and revealing skills and abilities previously unseen by many. I actually became recognized for the value I brought the team. I eventually moved into positions of leadership and, with others, experienced some important wins, on and off the ball field. But it appeared that the impact of those earlier years had lingered. The experience of being overlooked had come roaring back. A colleague with years of seasoned experience as a leader once told me the thing he feared the most was being "irrelevant." Being sent to the bench, again, felt like my moment of irrelevance.

I get it. I am older. Young leaders have new ways and fresh approaches. I was part of the same transition as the builder generation we displaced. I had prepared myself for a coming change, but I also looked forward—offering what I had to others who could do it better. I am still committed to the adventure, and to going to new places for Christ. Up to this moment I had looked forward to my final years and a chance to play an important part of a mission or organization, advising, helping and empowering others. I am okay to play my part and not having to be in the lead. And just at the moment I felt I had finally discovered my actual contribution, I found myself once again… on the bench.

—Robert Grant

CONVERGENCE

The hands of the Potter are still very much at work in the end-game, molding and shaping this stage in the journey just as actively as He was shaping the early days of faith. There is never a time He stops the formation process. Day in and day out he presses in, creating new contours of beauty—molding each of our lives into something far greater than we ever imagined. This third major chapter of His shaping work—the Convergence stage of a Christ-follower's development—reveals new insights and new deeds yet to be displayed. The Finishing Transition serves as a bridge for each of us to experience a convergent life and to hear the words, *"well done good and faithful servant"* (Matthew 25).

If you stand in the middle of a train track, between the two rails, you will notice that the space between them is greater than the width of your body. But as you look down the long, straight path of track in front of you, you will notice that it appears to become more narrow the farther it goes. Eventually, it looks as though the two rails come together—they converge—into just one rail.

Convergence brings together the two main "rails" on which life has been running—**who** God has shaped a Christ-follower to be (being) and **what** God has shaped them to do (doing). It is a new season of life, different from earlier days of calling and the mid-life demands and complexities. It is the realization that one's greatest act of worship is to simply be one's self.

Convergence is not man made. It is instigated and empowered by God and occurs in the life of both the homemaker and the lawyer, the farmer and the pastor. It occurs in the lives of those in the marketplace and those in vocational ministry. We all have the potential to experience Convergence, whether we feel that we have much or little to offer.

The path leading into Convergence is typically different than many of us have planned. Whether one has a passion to do the end-game well, or whether one feels paralyzed by the uncertainty ahead, transition moments take Christ-followers from where they are, to the next place in their discipleship. Ahead, the "train tracks" begin to merge. There are surprises, new paradigms and changes ahead. Just as it was true for Robert, it will be true for you. You are in a transition.

Could it be that the feeling of being "benched" or set-aside is a signal that the King is initiating something new—a time when less is more, where influence can be made without the requirement of a position, and when influence has more to do with who you are, than all the things you do or possess?

Could it be that the confusion and uncertainty one experiences around the topic of "retirement" be more about God moving an individual beyond the things they *can* do to a new place and a new way to engage those few things they *must* do?

And could it be that the culture has masked God's real purposes for this stage of life with a false scenario of something called "retirement"—portraying it as a time when you let others carry on with life as you are left alone to indulge?

What lies ahead is not the end, but may be the most strategic days of our lives if we choose to have eyes to see and ears to hear. Without the Finishing Transition, many Christ-followers often drift back to what they know to be more secure, as opposed to seeking God's purposes in new ways. God often uses all of life's circumstances—both good and difficult—to reveal that there is more to our stories, and that something new is commencing. The Convergence chapter does not mean the end, but rather, the beginning. New adventures lie just ahead.

PRECURSORS TO CONVERGENCE

What can one expect from this third chapter in the life of a Christ-follower, and what are some of the characteristics of life as one moves into a time of Convergence? Here are some important shifts that often take place.

1. Less is More

Many could read the word Convergence and understand it as a call to do and produce more—a zenith and time of high capacity in one's career. But in reality, Convergence is often about doing less while having greater Kingdom impact. **Less** activity that is **more** focused, intentional and strategic and that takes important wisdom and insights to new people and new places. Convergence is about focusing on those few important things one *must* do, as opposed to the many things one *can* do. In most instances it means doing the fewer "best" things that better leverage all of what God has entrusted to a Christ-follower.

The process of synthesizing the many things into the few things is often one of the core purposes of the Finishing Transition. It requires a look back to identify the unique ways God has shaped a life, and then a synthesis of those insights into a more focused delivery of life and ministry. While we live in a culture that esteems bigger and better, a Christ-follower now will be fulfilled by choosing to do the few things that could make the greatest difference rather than trying to do everything. Sometimes this involves pursuing new options or opportunities that have yet to be explored, or by taking on key tasks and heading down new paths leading to new adventures. It can also mean heading down familiar paths, but with greater focus—offering wisdom to those few who need it most. New or different paths are often required in the pursuit of better expressing one's contribution. Taking on the new is not just about enjoying new experiences, but is also about recognizing a critical way to offer resources, abilities, insights or financial help to a place or person that possess a Kingdom need. It becomes more about sacrificing what you have to meet a Kingdom opportunity.

As I coach many through the Finishing Transition, I often challenge a Christ-follower to see God's shaping work in new ways, and then to set themselves free beyond their current paradigms, duties and loyalties that have consumed their life, energy and focus to-date.

2. Influence Without Position

It is possible to have impact without position. The delivery of influence that God has shaped into a life requires looking at one's life vocation differently. One's *role* describes the influence one offers. For many years, we define who we are by our job or life assignment.

"I am a doctor."

"I am a homemaker."

"I am a teacher."

At some point soon, one's job or position will change or cease. Though employment days often end, the role one plays in the lives of others need not. Knowing one's role is about understanding the contribution one makes to others, and to our world. Role helps to unlock places where one can serve, and helps with decisions, options and opportunities that could be exercised. Influence occurs regardless of job or position. Jesus had no position, yet had the greatest of all influence. Our culture has led us to believe that influence comes from position. Therefore, when one lacks position, they feel they are unable to bring about influence. This has often served to fuel the dilemma around the purpose of "retirement." Distinguishing between a person's **job** and their **role** often sets a person free to move into what's next.

3. Encumbrances

> *"... let us throw off everything that hinders and the sin that so easily entangles. And let us run with perseverance the race marked out for us, fixing our eyes on Jesus, the pioneer and perfecter of faith." (Hebrews12:1-2)*

To run, finish and win a race, runners remove anything that could hold them back. Many things could be taken to the finish, but only a few things are actually needed. Convergence is about focus and intentionality. It's about being you and being present—trusting who God has made you to be and what God has shaped you to do. It's about shedding all the things you can do, and moving toward the finish line with the few things you must do. Life and ministry often straps onto us expectations, false demands and lies from the enemy that entangle our run. The Finishing Transition involves shedding that excess baggage and working through issues from the past that can (and will) hold each of us back.

Our pathology that follows us throughout our life finds some of its greatest formation in those early years—from ages 1-12. Some of the encumbrances that come aboard in those early years come back and stumble us in the latter years. The Finishing Transition will sometimes re-visit issues stemming from parents, siblings, environment, location, schooling, economic status, childhood events, and even times of abuse and hurt to help shed those things that can hold us back. Sometimes, things get placed in our bags that we are unaware of until we take a closer examination.

After the early years, life begins to build on those memories and reinforce things that were said or beliefs that were held. Along the way, we sometimes stop hoping to sort things out. Our salvation encounter with Christ provides the power to heal and redeem those experiences, but some of the hurt and early translation we have been given by others can still remain. Distortions are often reinforced by an enemy who will do anything—including hurt and oppress those we love—to sidetrack our journey with Christ. Many fall in the mid-game, under the load and the memories. In the second-half of life and our journey with Christ, God calls each of us deeper in our intimacy with Him so that we have both the trust and the faith as the work of stripping off the vestiges of our past continues.

4. Deeper Trust

Trust will always be at the center of our journey in Christ. Life in Christ is always about the deepening of trust, and it will always return back to our acceptance of His love. Transitions test the resolve of both. The Finishing Transition is a call for deeper trust at the end. There are still many things to know and even skills to learn, but it is possible (at times) to do life and ministry under the illusion that they can be done without consultation from God. While obvious in its error, many have gotten to this point in the journey with a heavy reliance on natural abilities and past experience, as opposed to a growing trust and confidence in God. Ambition comes face-to-face with alignment. Though our intimacy with Christ is always paramount to our life in Him, the end-game often involves another call to surrender to God's shaping work. At stake is spiritual authority—the presence of God in the life of men and women that more fully trust Him. During Convergence, position and titles often go away. It will be the spiritual authority that comes from greater abiding in Christ—living a life of alignment and surrender—that will produce the power of life-change in others.

5. Lifelong

All of life is the source of influence.

Down through the years the discipling of a Christ-follower produces a contribution and a fruit that reveals the love of God in ways that words alone cannot. It takes the Gospel and puts flesh on it like Christ did when He took on flesh and moved into the neighborhood (John 1, The Message). It is a fruit of the people, events and circumstances that have been experienced over the lifetime of a Christ-follower. The question is whether the fruit remains (John 15:5). Will the net result of our influence be one that fades with the fads of our days, or will it stand the test of time? The answer is in the "abiding." Abiding in Christ is a by-product of an ever-deepening walk with God, and a spiritual authority that man cannot buy or produce out of natural abilities.

The lifelong journey calls for alignment and response to God's ongoing shaping work, and it includes times of hardship, pride, rebellion and wounding. It may come as a surprise but it is often the wounding and failures that produce some of our future contribution. Our woundings—experiences that we hope to never experience again, and that should never happen to another—are often the seedbed for our most important influence in the future

6. Response Matters

Convergence is a by-product of God's ongoing, discipling work in the life of a believer. It is not something we can create, control or contrive. As the believer aligns with God's shaping work, the reality of Convergence unfolds. It speaks to a coordinated movement that can only be engineered by our Creator-God. It involves rivers coming together, experiences having new meaning, and what once seemed not important now moves to center stage. Convergence brings together who a person is with what a person has been shaped to do. Our responsibility is not to invent our future but to align with God's orchestrated work. As He shapes our lives in this stage of our journey, our response still matters.

THE POINT?

The purpose of the Finishing Transition is to move a Christ-follower into a time of Convergence and ultimate contribution. Up ahead is the next stage in one's development, life, and ministry. The adventure continues.

But how does one know they have entered into the Finishing Transition? And what does it look like to navigate the Finishing Transition?

The next chapters tell the story of Robert Grant—a friend and ministry partner to many—as he journeyed through the Finishing Transition. As you take this journey with Robert and myself, look for the common threads, emotions and insights as God challenges you to approach your future in new ways.

WANT MORE?

Here is a link to Leader Breakthru's website that will take you further on topics covered in this chapter:

www.leaderbreakthru.com/convergence

PART TWO

the bridge

Therefore, since we are surrounded by such a great cloud of witnesses, let us throw off everything that hinders and the sin that so easily entangles. And let us run with perseverance the race marked out for us.

—HEBREWS 12:1

> *It is not what we take up, but what we give up, that makes us rich.*[17]
>
> —HENRY WARD BEECHER

WHAT'S AHEAD?

Chapters 4-9 provide a running narrative of a Finishing Transition. They feature the 18-month transition of Robert Grant, a friend and ministry colleague. Our coaching conversations are approximated and they transpired over the course of a year. Robert was 71 years young at the time of these discussions. His transition could share some similarities to what you are experiencing as you journey through this time of in-between en route to a time of Convergence.

4

stepping back

> "We do not find our true self by seeking it.
> Rather we find it by seeking God."[18]
>
> —DAVID BRENNER

> I have made you and I will carry you;
> I will sustain you and I will rescue you.
>
> —ISAIAH 46:4

PHASE ONE—ENTRY

Coaching the Finishing Transition

I met Robert Grant during an event I was doing for the organization in which he was serving. He sat back like a seasoned veteran wondering what this "new guy" could bring to the mix that he did not already know or experience. My topic that day was to introduce coaching. The farther we went into the discussion, the more he leaned forward with interest. After my sessions he came up and we talked further. Though he spent much of his time helping younger leaders, he was impacted by the language and the definitions I shared around coaching.

As Robert and I met up at several more events we began to strike up a friendship and dialogue. Among the topics we kicked around were those related to times of transition. It was becoming clear Robert was the midst of a transition. He was up against the challenges of finding his way through the Finishing Transition. One day, at one of our training events, we connected again and I could tell he had a question for me. He shared his take on his current circumstances, compared them to the insights I share in my book *Stuck!*, and then asked if I thought he was in a transition. I asked him what he thought. He looked back at me with a puzzled look. I was the "supposed" expert, yet I was asking him. He nodded affirmatively. He said he felt he had entered a time of transition awhile back, and he went further by identifying that it was clear to him he was in the Finishing Transition and that, quoting my book, he was "stuck."

After Robert shared, I told him that based on what I had heard, I agreed. I also agreed that he had probably entered into the transition a few months back. He was in the in-between. He then asked if I would consider coaching him through this time. I told him I would be honored.

And so our coaching of his Finishing Transition began.

"Hey Robert, glad we are finally connecting. I am excited about our time together and the chance to walk through this thing called a transition."

"I am also excited Terry," Robert stated, "and a little fascinated

stepping back

about how this will all work. I have mentored and coached others, but I have not had many coaches or conversations like the ones we are headed into."

"I get that, and you are not the first." I replied. "I coach a lot of people who help others gain clarity and focus, and yet their own development falls into the important-yet-not-urgent basket." I continued. "Let me first make sure that we share the definition of coaching. I believe that good coaching draws insights out, whereas mentoring seeks to place new insights within." Robert was nodding as he remembered the training we had conducted and the impact the clarity of definitions had brought to his understanding of both skills.

"Coaching a transition is primarily about helping you process this unique time in your journey, and discern how God is at work using this in-between moment to move you into the next stage of your development. I am going to adopt a coaching posture for most of our time. Periodically though, I will offer insights and concepts related to personal development that could be helpful. Those will be mentoring moments, but you will quickly see me returning back to coaching, helping you process that new information. How's all that sound to you?"

I paused to make sure we were both clear about the expectations for our coaching conversations. Robert was quick to give the affirmative signal.

"One final note as we get started," I continued, "I am going to be using the *Transition Life Cycle* (p. 24) and the *IDEA Coaching Pathway*[19] to help guide our conversations. They will be in the background of our time, helping to inform our conversations. You will set the agenda for our calls, but they will offer help. All of this means that our goal is to help you process what the Spirit of God is doing and the issues that you are up against. As you walk through this important moment in your journey, you call the shots. I will do all I can to help you hear yourself and better recognize what God might be saying to you. That is my primary role as your coach."

"I get it Terry," Robert commented. "And I appreciate the chance to process all that I am going through. I know I am going to need your insight and expertise related to all of this. I am not quite sure what I need to be talking about. All I know is that I am in a different time, and the more I have tried to figure it out on my own, the more confused and frustrated things have become."

"No worries friend. I believe God is at work in what you are sensing and feeling, and that together we can help you recognize what God might be doing!" I responded. I have learned over my many years of coaching experience that, no one gets to clarity alone.

"Let's dive in and see where we are before our time is up today!" I began. "Tell me about what you have been experiencing."

For the next 15-20 minutes Robert began to give me an overview of his journey to-date, and then he described the previous 12 months. As is true for many in a transition, the more Robert talked about his time of transition, the more feelings of restlessness and new questions filled the air. In particular to the Finishing Transition, he was feeling like ministry was passing him by. Although he was ready and able to contribute, somehow he was being sent to "the bench" and others were taking over the tasks he once was called on to perform. It was like he was being passed over, yet his hand was up, offering to be of help. He did not want to believe that the question of age had finally caught up with him. It was hard to not let some resentment and bitterness take hold, but thus far he was fighting the good fight, and seeking to believe the best. After hearing his story, I asked Robert a few important entry-oriented questions.

"So what do you think God is doing in all of this?" I asked. "How do you see him using this time to shape you?"

Robert thought for a few moments then responded. "I think that God wants me to take a step back. I have been involved in many things, seen God do some amazing things, been around all types of leaders and have served in a series of assignments and movements. I am thankful for all He has done, but right now He is slowing things down so that I can get my hands around the bigger picture." Robert continued. "Things are obviously coming to a standstill for a reason. It is hard to feel like you've been sidelined. But I know that He is wanting to speak to me, and to use this moment. I think I need to spend time looking at what has gotten me here, and what signals I might have missed along the way."

"Sounds good Robert. I think you are on the right track. It is hard to lean into an unknown, but my guess is that the more you acknowledge that God is at work, the greater the capacity you will have to see His work." I replied. "But let me follow this all up with another question—what if you are done, Robert? What if God is doing something new, and that your days within the organization are coming to an end? That might be why He has initiated this transition. Think about that, and then talk about what that might mean."

This time there was a longer pause from Robert.

"Well, I guess I am hoping that scenario is not the case. I still believe in this ministry and in the contribution I am making. I don't really want to think that I could be done—that there is a chance my time here is coming to an end. That kind of thinking would have a lot of ramifications for my family and my future. At this point, I haven't really given that much consideration. Are you saying that is what is happening?"

"No! At this point I am not saying or concluding anything. It is way too early in your transition for that kind of conclusion. But what I am getting at with the question is that it is important to take that step back right now and let God have free rein to do His work and reveal His purposes. He is obviously at work, and is seeking to take you to the next stage in your development. I do think it is important to give Him room to work."

"I think you are right," responded Robert. "This is a transition moment, and if I want to know what God is doing, I must allow Him the freedom to work. It's just hard to entertain the thought."

Robert's response is one of the reasons I said yes to his request for coaching. He is a good leader, has his opinions, but is honest. And at his core he is committed to following God, and living a life of surrender. He has modeled that life for Christ-followers and leaders all over the country and through several generations.

"Robert I think this is a good stopping point." I announced. "What action step would you like to take as a result of our discussion today? And what was most helpful from our first time together?"

"I think those are one-in-the-same, Terry. I think what was most helpful is actually tied to my action step. I realize I need to take a step back, and get a bigger view of what is occurring right now in my journey, and I need to work on that before our next time together. I think I need to set aside some time to reflect on my journey and take a look at how God has been at work."

"Sounds good Robert." I said, "and I think there's a way I can help. How about I send you a link and instructions on how to make a Post-it Note Timeline of your journey. This tool will help you see your life from that big-picture point of view. It will take about two-hours to complete, but will help you achieve exactly what you are needing. Can you have it ready to share the next time we are together?" I asked.

"You got it Terry, I'll work on it between now and our next coaching time and bring it with me and be ready to share."

Robert and I closed in prayer and set up our next coaching appointment.

ENTRY PHASE—THE ISSUES

1. The Finishing Transition often involves separating influence from position. It is not uncommon that one's vocational position comes to an end as part of the transition. God is often using this change to signal that identity and influence are two separate issues. Men and women are both impacted by this, but men often more so. For men, identity is more commonly tied to what they do. Who they are and the potential for influence is often tied to their job.

2. The Finishing Transition is often signals an ending and a beginning. It is a time when God begins the process of synthesizing all that has transpired into an understanding of one's unique and ultimate contribution. Therefore, big-picture perspective is essential. Most of us don't realize all that God has woven into our lives until we stop, and take a look back.

3. Entry into the Finishing Transition often carries with it a heightened state of emotions. Stepping away from what is

known often means stepping away from friends and all that is familiar. Moving forward often means seeing life differently and with new paradigms. Stepping into the end-game brings the baggage of "growing old" and experiencing (for the first time) the labels given to others—"seniors," "elderly," and "retired." Remember: finishing does not mean finished.

ROBERT'S REFLECTION

Entering into the Finishing Transition for me was like riding on a roller coaster. Ministry had become quite a ride: filled with many thrills, many ups and downs and the need for more speed. As lead pastor of a growing church I experienced some thrilling experiences. Lives were being changed as many people came to Christ and were growing in Christ. God blessed us with new buildings, new programs and new staff members that allowed us to build bridges to our community.

However, I began to experience not only the highs of ministry, but also the lows. The many demands and responsibilities of leading began to have serious consequences. I became very driven by all of the tasks on my daily to-do list. I began to live in a perpetual state of hurry. Living for the applause of many became my default and ongoing motivation. I was saying yes to everyone and everything, which only accelerated an already maddening pace.

This maddening pace was one I knew I couldn't continue. It was having an adverse effect on my relationships. My wife and children were gracious to me regarding the amount of time I was spending in the name of ministry for God, but I knew that something was wrong as I continued to live a driven life. My mentors and partners in ministry also realized I was burning the proverbial candle at both ends. I found myself at odds with those who loved me and truly cared for me. Relational conflict with those around me became a common occurrence and physical exhaustion began to set in.

The biggest struggle for me was the nagging awareness that my intimacy with Christ had waned. The joy and peace that I had experienced in Christ was no longer there. Instead, I found myself alone and distant not only from people but from Christ. A restlessness began to settle in like a low-grade fever; the life-giving relationship with Christ that I preached and encouraged had become a theory rather than a reality in my own journey. The Word of God had become merely a tool to help others instead of bread for my own soul.

I found myself wanting to get off the roller coaster. I realized something wasn't right. I realized I was riding on one rail instead of two: the rail of doing. I knew that I couldn't continue to ride only on the rail of doing without crashing. It was the pace of ministry and the inevitable depletion of adrenaline that left me leading on empty.

WANT MORE?

Here is a link to Leader Breakthru's website that will take you further on topics covered in this chapter:

www.leaderbreakthru.com/timeline

5

rearview mirror

Radical obedience to Christ is not easy. It's not comfort, not health, not wealth, and not prosperity in this world. Radical obedience to Christ risks losing all these things. But in the end, such risk finds its reward in Christ. And he is more than enough for us.[20]

—DAVID PLATT

PHASE TWO—EVALUATION

Grappling with Finishing

> *I have long believed that we each have a purpose to which we have been called in Christ to fulfill. So what was driving the unrest and disconnect I was experiencing? It seemed that I was "fading" rather than "fulfilling." Regardless of how clear I was in my own self-understanding, this transition was unsettling me at a deep level of my soul. I don't want to "feel" retired. I am convinced that I am in the best place in my life to make a significant contribution based on my gifts, wisdom and experience. But I now face the potential loss of influence.*
>
> — Robert Grant

Over a month passed between our first and second coaching appointments. Robert was ready. With his Post-it Note Timeline in front of him and insights ready to share, it was clear that our coaching was moving into a time of discovery as we further unpacked Robert's story. We were moving into a time of evaluation. Issues from his past would come to shed light on the present but also provide guideposts that pointed into the future.

"So Robert, tell me how things have been since we last talked, and how things are going, especially in light of the transition."

"Things are good, Terry. Since we talked last I think I have settled more into the reality that I am in a transition, and that God is at work using this time to speak into my life. I had an incredible experience creating and reflecting on my timeline. That is a powerful tool."

"Yes it is, Robert. I use my Post-it Note Timeline as the core tool to help me maintain perspective. Christ-followers who finish well are able to live their lives from a big-picture, lifetime perspective. Before we dive into your timeline and you share your story, what is one big insight you had as you looked at your life in this manner? Overall, what did you see?"

"I think the one thing that stuck out to me more than any other is the number and impact of relationships I have had down through the years," Robert shared. "I have had the privilege of working in many settings, made many friends, and I have had the privilege of ministering to many people, from different tribes, and have witnessed God's faithfulness in their lives down through the years. It has been truly significant."

"That is significant Robert!" I stated. "You have identified a pattern in terms of how God has both shaped and grown your influence through relationships. Tell me more."

Robert proceeded to review the five major chapters in his development, each focused around a series of relationships and assignments. His early years involved roles within a variety of ministries, each netting lessons about how to do ministry, and the type of people God calls us to be. It was powerful to just sit back and listen to his stories and memories being relived.

We talked through the key turning points in Robert's journey, and how each centered around ministries in which he participated, and how the lessons he learned advanced his view of God, and his view of himself. Somewhere in the midst of this sharing, we began to delve more deeply into what Robert's past was saying to him related to his own identity and his current situation in the Finishing Transition.

I asked Robert for his reflections about each of these significant ministry assignments and what were some of the key lessons about who he was and how God had shaped him to influence others.

"I can now see why much of my orientation and identity comes from my work. And it now makes more sense as to why I felt destabilized during our last coaching conversation when you asked me to let go of my hold on my job. Most of my life I have served around or been part of some important ministries and movements. I have drawn some of my significance from what I was doing, and from who/what I was associated. While I feel good about much that has transpired, and those I have been able to rub shoulders with, I also recognize that it has crept over into how I have defined myself. I further recognized that how I felt about myself was tied (at times) to something that was making a difference. I was (and am) defined by much of that—more than I thought."

"Wow, Robert! That all is really significant insight. As you hear yourself saying all that, what stands out to you?" I asked.

"On the one hand, I feel like God allowed me to be a part of some of the best ministry experiences, and I am grateful. On the other hand, I also feel that I have been so loyal to those roles and ministries, that I may have exchanged some of my self-worth and identity for a sense of belonging. That last part does not feel good."

Things grew quiet as Robert reflected on his realization.

Like all of us, some of the best things about Robert had turned around and had now begun to work against him. His strength (true self) had also become a part of his weakness (false self).

"I am wondering Robert if this issue may be one of the key reasons God has initiated this time of transition. Could it be that the false side of this strength might be holding you back from moving into the future and experiencing God's best in the days ahead?" As Robert pondered my thoughts, I shared one more.

"I could see that my challenge last time about your current ministry position may be coming to end, rattled you. That was not my purpose. But I did sense that the Holy Spirit could be signaling an issue He wants to address. And as I listened to you share today, I see a thread of loyalty running throughout your timeline. Honor, loyalty, servanthood, perseverance and commitment to the team are some of the finest of values as a minister. But these qualities, if they go too far, could begin to supplant your identity in Christ. This could keep you from continuing to move forward into new assignments that better deliver who Christ has shaped you to be."

These two deep insights would take time for Robert to process. I was not seeking to convince Robert, but rather making my first attempt in helping him to synthesize his insights from his past into potential guides during his current transition.

"How do you want me to react to all this Terry?" was Robert's immediate response.

"Any way you want Robert!" I replied. "My desire is to help you process what might be occurring, and not to fix you. I could be off in the connecting of these dots. I actually believe you already have insight as to what God is doing, and better insights than me in terms of what is occurring. Feel free to process this any way you want!"

"Well first off, I think this is spot on." replied Robert. "I am not sure what it all means yet, but it is clear to me that we are onto something important. And I can see its relevance to what I am facing now. My identity can often be too much in play when it comes to my role in the ministry. When I look back on my life, and see it from the big-picture, I always seem to come face-to-face with questions related to my self-worth and value. I love Christ. He is my Lord, Savior and King. I am His and He is mine. Done deal. Settled issue. And yet at times, I have clung to position and place because I have wondered about my value. If I no longer had position, what would that mean and would they still want me to be a part?"

It was quiet.

I let Robert process all that was running through his mind.

He was hearing the voice of the Shepherd—something more important than his own voice. After a few moments, I broke the silence.

"So, where do we go next with this Robert? How do you want to respond?"

"I think I want to take this home and reflect on it more. I want my wife Sue to speak into this. I want some time to pray things through, and spend time letting the Spirit lead me through the reality of this truth. Is that all right, Terry?"

"Absolutely! Are you kidding? I am incredibly proud of you for going this far. This is big stuff, and I believe it is vital for your future. Take all the time you need. I am in this for you."

"I am on this Terry! This is not me trying to sidestep what God is at work doing. I feel like we are making significant progress. The timeline exercise unlocked some things for me. I believe that I could have never gotten here without your help and questions. I believe we are on the right track."

"So what was most helpful today from our time?" I asked Robert.

"It was those comments that linked all this together. Before today my various roles and assignments were independent from each other. But seeing all of them together in a larger picture was a key that I think just might have helped me unlock my future."

Robert and I closed in prayer, giving thanks for the Holy Spirit's work during our time. Together we asked God to continue to work and help Robert's ongoing insight.

EVALUATION PHASE—THE ISSUES

1. The Finishing Transition is about "connecting the dots." It's about discovering how God is weaving the past together with the present, and clarifying future contribution. Surfacing the backstory and inviting the Holy Spirit into the discernment process yields new insights and revelation. The focus is to realize one's ultimate contribution. Transitions are best processed using the rearview mirror.

2. The Finishing Transition seeks to identify major themes and patterns God has shaped into an individual for influence. These have occurred over one's lifetime. Whether people, cause or function, past assignments produce a set of core passions that begin to reveal one's contribution. It is this that they will pass onto others.

3. The Evaluation segment of the Finishing Transition requires a Christ-follower to embrace the reality of their story. Seeing what has occurred helps to reveal what might occur in the future. Integrity checks, obedience checks, divine contacts and the Word of God continue to speak into one's life and shed light on one's future path.

ROBERT'S REFLECTION

Prevenient Grace

As my coaching continued, I increasingly recognized where God was at work in my life prior to this transition, and how my past was influencing how I was responding to what was presently occurring. The discoveries from gaining a big-picture, sovereign point-of-view of my life brought a new desire to yield to God's presence and work in the transition. As I began recalling past moments and encounters, I started to see my identity being shaped and patterns of behavior that were now part of the fabric of my personality. These discoveries and my past contributions have continued to carry forward. There were also some painful experiences that I had yet to process and learn from. Nothing is wasted in God's economy. Recognizing these patterns is key to being able to understand what significant influence might look like in the future, and in making sure I don't repeat behaviors that could hold me back. Once again, coaching was the key. Terry's question seemed to continue to unlock issues I could not get to on my own. The more I was able to see God's work in my past through the Post-it Note Timeline, the more I discovered the need for greater resolution with my past before I moved into the future with health. It is divine grace that precedes decisions that I need to make in the days ahead.

WANT MORE?

Here is a link to Leader Breakthru's website that will take you further on topics covered in this chapter:

lbu.leaderbreakthru.com/products/ten-ways-god-builds-character

6
a timely word

In our abandonment we give ourselves over to God just as God gave Himself for us. The consequences of abandonment never enter into our outlook because our life is taken up in Him.[21]

—OSWALD CHAMBERS

The condition of an enlightened mind is a surrendered heart.[22]

—ALAN REDPATH

PHASE TWO—EVALUATION

Grappling with the Finishing Transition

My Finishing Transition was amplified by the national role in which I was serving suddenly drawing to a close—putting me in an unexpected internal struggle with issues of meaning and worth. Suddenly, I was in the dark. The suddenness surprised me.

We tend to not like being in the dark, and most of us do not like sitting in the silence. We can't see where we are going and we begin to realize that we have lost control. I can't control my future nor predict its outcomes. Wisdom from scripture to trust in God's superintending presence is my need. But when disorientation arrived, with major change waiting in the wings, I recognized that my next steps were important.

— *Robert Grant*

Robert and I had spent time connecting around other things, but he emailed me one day and said he was ready for our next coaching conversation. As I prepared for our session, I surrendered myself to the Spirit and His agenda for our time. It was clear this would be an important call.

"Hey Coach, how you doing?"

"I am good, Robert. How about yourself?" I replied.

"Good and thankful for a chance to reconnect and take all this further. I have a lot to talk about."

Robert and I spent the first minutes catching up and creating a sense of safety for our conversation. When you coach, you are coaching a person, not their problem. In the age of information and instant answers, coaching is some of the most important ministry of our day.

"So, catch me up to speed since our last call, and our significant time we had together," I stated. I knew Robert was ready to talk.

"I have had a lot of good time to reflect and spend time with the Lord around all that we have talked about," he began. "It was just what I needed. This has hit me all so suddenly that I feel like I have been walking in the dark up to now. Our previous conversations, and the Post-it Note Timeline have given me fresh eyes as I have gone deeper in processing what I am feeling and experiencing. I had some great time with Sue and she helped give me perspective as well. I feel like I finally have some order to my thoughts. It's been good, and I am thankful."

"That is great my friend. I know that all of this stuff feels like it is swirling around and needs to be solved, but God is not in a hurry. The process of discovery is the key to helping you find the answers you need, but will also create ownership for the future direction you are seeking," I responded.

"In our session today, I think I would like to talk about some things that surfaced during my Timeline reflection. Somehow this all is linked together with my ability to better understand how God is working," continued Robert. "Would it be okay to start there?"

"Absolutely, Robert," I responded, "you set the agenda for this time, and I will follow you."

Robert began to talk about a few past ministry experiences that he had spent time reflecting on. These experiences involved encounters Robert had with leaders from the various organizations that he had served. It was important for him to verbalize those various situations and highlight some of the issues he recognized in his past. Articulation is often key to focus. The more we can hear ourselves put words to the situations we have faced, the greater the opportunity for those experiences to come into focus.

It became clear that a pattern of hurt was emerging from the various experiences Robert was recounting. One event in particular captured threads of what he had found throughout many of the situations he had experienced. This event involved a series of experiences that had hurt him, and caused him to question his role and to doubt his value as a leader. As Robert continued to share, it was obvious that this situation was still having an impact all these years later. It was festering underneath—tied to his view of himself and his work. His role he played and his view of his own identity remained connected. As he concluded his remarks and the overall series of experiences from his past, he asked me what I was hearing.

"First off," I began, "your willingness to go deeper in all of this and trust me with some of your deepest moments in ministry is amazing. It's not easy to go back and relive some of the experiences you have gone through in the past.

"My first question is, as you review the tapes and the impact of these experiences, what's standing out to you? It seems you shared each of these accounts because you sense that they are important and are trying to tell you something. What do you think they are saying?"

Robert paused and thought for a few minutes before sharing.

"Well, first off I thought you were going to give me all the answers, but we both know by now that would never happen." We both laughed. "My best guess is that each of these came up because they were more than just difficult experiences for me. Each seem to be speaking to the feeling I have about being 'benched', and my inability to come to terms with my job potentially ending."

"Important stuff, Robert," I responded. "Keep going."

"I don't know where else to go with all this." Robert continued.

"Yes you do Robert," I challenged. "What might each of these, together, be telling you? And in particular, what does that one incident say to you? It sounded like that was particularly difficult for you?"

"My guess would be that these events impacted how I see myself. My struggle to understand my self-worth is still being impacted by all that has happened in the past."

"What if I say to you that you have not brought closure to that event? How would you react to the reality that more work needs to be done to bring closure to this past event and the hurt that occurred?"

We had hit a nerve.

Robert's visceral response was the obvious clue that though many years had passed, and efforts had been made to move forward, he remained without resolution.

Robert just sat there, and shook his head. "Man, I thought I had worked through all of this! I can't believe I am back here again. Are you sure we have to drudge all this back up and look at it?"

"No, I am not sure that it all needs to be gone over again." I replied. "But what I am sure of is that you have not brought closure to that experience. I know that, because the wounding that occurred back then is having a direct impact on you today. It feels like your Finishing Transition is not just about a potential job change. This could be about overcoming obstacles that could hold back your future and all that God has for you!" I paused, then shared my summation of what I believe this situation could mean.

"Robert, you are a loyal, valiant warrior! You are the type of individual and leader anyone would want to go to war with and fight alongside. But loyalty to the organization you serve, or to the leaders you follow might actually be the things that keep you from discovering and living out your unique and ultimate contribution. Let me state something I am sure you know. What defines you is your intimate relationship with Christ, who He has made you to be, and your identity in Him. Your ability to touch the lives of others, regardless of the organizational jobs you have held or the movements you are part of, have been the sourced of your identity for who you are in Christ."

Once again, all was quiet.

"Robert there is a tool that God often uses to shape His followers. It is called Negative Preparation. It is when God allows difficult things to happen to good people. His allowance is not because He is powerless to change that situation, or because He does not care. What is at work is something greater. Sometimes we are loyal to a fault and our commitment to others gets in the way of our commitment to Christ and His purposes for us in the future. In Negative Preparation, God sets us free to move onto more of what He has for our lives. It could be that He is setting you free from what has occurred in your past in order to move you into a time of freedom and finishing well."

Robert looked up as if he had finally seen the daylight.

For the first time the dots had connected and he was able to see his identity in a new way—more deeply rooted in Christ.

"Terry, these words are so timely. They resonate inside of me and bring clarity to the reflections I have done over these past few weeks.

I knew I needed to break free, and there was a depth of hurt that was underneath what was occurring, but I couldn't see it this clearly and I didn't know what to do about it. It is incredible to have someone who cares, and is willing to listen and walk with you in all that you are facing." Robert sighed in deep relief.

"So I guess our key word for this session is 'closure.' My question is, how can I bring closure to all this so I can move forward? What's my next step?"

I responded, "I've got a suggestion for you that others have found to be helpful as they sought to break free from past experiences. I think it might be helpful for you."

"I am all ears, Terry. What is it?"

"It's called a Closure Paper!" I continued. "I am not talking about a huge document, or many months of work. Rather, it's a 2-3 page summary of the lessons you learned, the lies that you believed and the longings of your heart as you move into the future. You'll want to include the ways you'll need to think and the ways you'll need to behave in the days ahead that will help you better align with how God has shaped you."

"I like it Terry! It sounds challenging, but doable. It feels like I might finally be able to move on from that experience, and be able to better handle what's ahead of me. I think I am going to need some help with what the paper should look like if I am going to be able to complete the task."

"How about I email you my template for the closure paper. It will include helpful tips to get you ready for our next coaching conversation." (*See Appendix for the Closure Paper Template*)

"The bottom line here Robert is that our inability to bring closure to our past experiences often makes it difficult for us to move into the future. I have found this to be particularly true in the Finishing Transition. The enemy will do everything he can to put roadblocks en route to finishing well. One of his strategies is to surface lies we came to believe in our past and then camp on them—trying to sabotage our growth and the steps leading to convergence."

"I can't tell you how much all this means to me, Terry. Your ability to ask me the questions and challenge me to go after what I knew was there has offered me the first signs of hope I have felt in some time. Thank you!"

"You are welcome Robert. This is why God takes each of us into times of transition. He surfaces issues holding us back, and brings closure to the issues that need to be dealt with, in order to move us from where we are to where He wants us to go. It's great to be along for the ride."

Once again, Robert and I closed in prayer.

ALIGNMENT PHASE—THE ISSUES

1. The Finishing Transition often forces us to revisit issues from our past. New ways to look at old problems is often the work of the Spirit who seeks to heal and lead us into the truth about ourselves (John 16:33). Without this work, the gifts, insights and values that have been entrusted to us by God to share with others often remain locked up inside us.

2. The Finishing Transition involves a series of shifts in our paradigms in order to finish well. Past assignments and experiences have netted who we are and how God has shaped us to minister. Breaking free from past wounds and patterns of thought requires an act of surrender and alignment to God's forming work. The prize of surrender is revelation.

3. The Alignment segment in the Finishing Transition often involves the help of another. Though each of us has access to the same resources, we can lose sight of how best to apply the truth and power of God to our lives. We do not get to clarity alone. It takes courage to bring someone along with you as you make this journey. Someone coming alongside of you often makes all the difference.

ROBERT'S REFLECTION

The Quiver

As I began to experience the potential of new purpose and vision, my wife shared an insight from ancient scripture that gave me a word picture and refocused my view of my current situation. The ancient writer spoke poetically of a finely tuned, sharpened arrow that is placed in the quiver of an archer. The quiver remained by his side containing precision-based projectiles, ready when needed by the archer. When that time came, and the arrow was drawn from the quiver, it would be called upon to make an exacting impact as the archer sent it toward the desired target. This well-honed instrument was placed in the quiver in the darkness, hidden from others. In the silence it is tucked away and remains at rest by the master archer's side until he calls on it, and propels it to its target.

Though I continued to struggle with being sent to the bench—discarded in the midst of my (potentially) greatest contribution—I now wait for a moment in time, honed and wondering when that might be, and what the challenge might be that I face. If this is what my God wants, then I serve. But I also wonder if God could be using this transition to help me better identify new ways to deliver the contribution He has shaped into my life.

Quietly, I remain in His quiver.

WANT MORE?

Here is a link to Leader Breakthru's website that will take you further on topics covered in this chapter:

lbu.leaderbreakthru.com/products/integration-being-doing

7
different

To stand before the Holy One of eternity is to change. Resentments cannot be held with the same tenacity when we enter his gracious light.[23]

—RICHARD J. FOSTER

PHASE FOUR—DIRECTION

The Way Forward in the Finishing Transition

> *There is a God-given desire in the heart of every person to be a difference-maker. We are made in God's image to contribute, and have been given special gifts—unique to who we are—that enable us to fulfill our calling and purpose. Living into God's design and stewarding these gifts enacts the healthy part of being a follower of Christ. There is a distinction, however, between "performing a task" and making "an authentic contribution." Performing carries the risk of pursuing ambition or significance. Authentic contribution involves gaining a healthy self-understanding and living into the best application of the gifts we have been given. As I continued to ponder what the coming years might hold, I providentially was introduced to the idea of coaching as a way forward. Suddenly, opportunity and lasting contribution seemed possible again. Merely performing tasks leads to a thirst that will never be satisfied, but Godly contribution satisfies all that is deep within.*
>
> *— Robert Grant*

As the months progressed, Robert's Finishing Transition moved beyond uncertainty to a new sense of clarity and hope. The more time he spent on issues related to Evaluation, the more he was able to recognize his need for surrender and greater alignment with God's forming work. The future had now begun to come into focus. It was time for our next coaching conversation.

"Hey Robert! How are you man? How goes the battle?"

"Things are good, Coach!" He replied. "I have been looking forward to our call today and to processing my Closure Paper with you. I have really valued this exercise, and can see now how much I needed to walk down this path."

"All that sounds good Robert." I said. "It feels like we have turned a corner. I can hear it in your voice. You sound more encouraged than you were earlier."

"I am. I think today I'd like to spend our time talking through what I've written and discovered as I walked through this exercise. I'd like to share some of the things I am thinking about when it comes to the future."

I gave Robert a the go-ahead and off we went into a review of his paper. You will remember that coming out of our last conversation he was to write a summation of the lessons, lies and longings that came from a difficult experience from his past, and to state some insights as well as his intended future behavior.

Robert reviewed his summation as well as his appreciation for how the Lord used these various opportunities to bring new growth and skills. He then moved into four key insights he felt he learned and how he wanted to behave differently in the future. The paper was three pages in length, and was well done.

The only problem was that it may not have gone far enough. Too often we generalize moments like these and do not have the courage to strike at the core of the issues involved. New behaviors come as a result of new paradigms and insights. That which changes us the most is tied to insights and lessons from our past. These new insights and behaviors become guardrails to keep us on track into the future. After Robert shared his thoughts, I moved to a series of questions.

"I think your summary insights are well done and are essential for the future. What do you think is your most important lesson coming from this situation? I find myself wondering if you have gone deep enough. What was God trying to teach you, and what new behavior do you need to adopt in the future in order to break this theme of misplaced identity you've discovered?"

As he has done before, Robert paused and reflected on my questions.

"I think honestly I cared too much about the positions I held. It became the source of my worth. In the future, I need to check myself and make sure I have accountable relationships around me that could call me out should I once again head in that direction."

"Good work, Robert. Having the courage to summarize what occurred gives you new ways to think about how to navigate the future."

Robert smiled at me knowing that more was coming. "But what am I missing?"

It was my turn to pause, and then I responded.

"How is this any different than what we already know? How does this actually take us beyond that past event, and help us overcome the obstacles that you once again have encountered? Don't hear me wrong. You are on the right track, but I want to challenge you to dig deeper into the lessons and insights you will need in the future. You game?"

"Yes." chimed Robert quickly, "but I would like to see if I can take a crack at it first before you give me your input. That could help me best." Robert responded.

"You bet," I said. "In fact, that is what we want. What you think and believe, Robert, is more important that any assessment or input I can give you."

Robert took a run at going deeper.

"I will never be able to control the actions and circumstances of others, and yet in my past I have given over my view of myself and my worth to others. I have remained loyal to the point that I have sacrificed who Christ has told me I am, in order to be what an organization wanted or needed me to be. This can no longer be. No longer can I give away that which others have no right to control."

Robert looked at me and I motioned for him to continue.

"In the future, I desire to be a faithful servant of Christ, a steward of my gifts and abilities, and do all I can to join others in order to best advance Christ's Kingdom. I will not serve solely to please others, to gain favor with others, to gain favor with the organization in which I serve, or to achieve the agenda of another just so I will be seen as a valued member of a team. I will filter my "yes" and "no" in the future by asking myself two things: (1) Am I saying yes to gain favor and/or to prove my value to others, and (2) does this opportunity move me closer to who I am (my identity) in Christ, or take me farther away?"

"Wow!" I exclaimed. "That was more than a 100% improvement. That is exactly what I was talking about, and now there is more depth to the real issue you are facing, and more certainty to your future behavior. What are your thoughts as you hear yourself laying it all out?"

"Before, it was theory. Now it is truth that can be translated into life. It feels good. And I can see why you have pushed me. As I think about my current situation, the loss of my role and the feeling of wandering in the dark, out of control, not seeing the events of my life, and how they will impact my future. And let me go farther, Terry. It's time. Things have dogged me for my entire journey, and it is this very issue that was creating the panic I felt even when we first began to talk. The issue of my value and worth may stay with me to the end, but I know now that it will not be what keeps me from finishing well."

"I think we have had a breakthrough Robert!" I responded. "It feels like we are standing on holy ground. And one of the most important aspects of this moment is that all of this came from you—your discovery of the depth of what you were up against, and the power of the Spirit breaking through with new clarity and fueling your passion to follow Christ to the end. Well done my friend."

We closed in prayer.

DIRECTION PHASE—THE ISSUES

1. The Finishing Transition often speaks to issues of identity and self-worth. Wounds that remain open impact one's ability to finish well. The end-game is a Christ-follower's "run to the tape," unhindered by past issues or sins which can so easily entangle us (Hebrews 12:1,2).

2. The Finishing Transition is not about doing many things. Finishing well is about focusing on those few things that make one's best Kingdom contribution. It's about doing less to do more. Messages from others often seek to communicate a different need, and to distort who we really are. Breaking free is often an act of surrender and alignment to God's forming work in your past.

3. The Direction segment in the Finishing Transition brings you closer to God's sovereign design for your life, and the good deeds He has created for you to do (Ephesians 2:10). Closure

involves more than just thinking differently about ourselves, but also involves behaving differently. Sometimes we must "behave our way" into the truth about who we are and our new place in the journey. The Christian life involves alternating moments where we must "trust" and "obey."

ROBERT'S REFLECTION
Moving Toward the Light

One night, in the early morning hours, I woke up with my pillow over my head. In the stillness and solitude of that moment, words came out of my mouth…"Jesus, you alone are enough." I knew in my heart of hearts that I meant what I was confessing. I was free from being defined by what I was able to do. I was content to be who I was, made in His image, with gifts unique to my calling and with a purpose God alone could define and deliver. I do not believe I was capable of getting to this juncture by myself. Foremost, I needed the voice of God speaking into my life. I needed the voice of a coach outside of my own head to keep me moving toward the light of God's voice. A coach is not a replacement for God speaking but a good coach can help dispel confusion, facilitate clarity about what God is saying and what we need to do about it.

Every opportunity and door that has opened now takes on a different meaning. Whether it is individual encounters or public speaking opportunities, there is new freedom to be a source of influence…or not. This does not neutralize initiative or good planning, but it is a freeing from the perilous pursuit of finding significance in the wrong places. What seemed to be "fading to grey" and becoming invisible is now moving toward me, and what lies ahead yields anticipation of doing His bidding according to His pleasure and timing. I am becoming at peace with silence and content with being invisible, as well as comfortable with opportunities that have a broad reach.

WANT MORE?

Here is a link to Leader Breakthru's website that will take you further on topics covered in this chapter:

www.leaderbreakthru.com/convergence

8

resolve

*Trust in the Lord with all your heart
and lean not on your own understanding.*

—PROVERBS 3:5

Never be afraid to trust an unknown future to a known God.[24]

—CORRIE TEN BOOM

The Hope of the Finishing Transition

> *Entering the age customarily assigned for "retirement" presents a unique challenge with few road maps. There are plenty of books, blogs and seminars out there, along with many voices calling for you to maximize your final days. Being successful during your primary years of career development can yield even more pressure. When you approach this season of life you are often not ready. Retirement is for those who are older and yet you feel that you are at an optimum place to make your best contribution. The reality of the end-game does not really set in until you reach that threshold and then it hits you as you face your most important transition. I did not need someone telling me what to do. I needed a path for gaining clarity and a safe relationship to stay in the journey with me until I got it—I needed the presence of a coach. Could it be that what I needed the most is what I have been shaped to offer others?*
>
> — *Robert Grant*

It was weeks before Robert and I connected again. He was busy and so was I. Life does not stop during times of transition. In fact, part of the pressure of a transition is that life and its many choices and decisions just keep coming. Robert called my office and we finally found a good time to connect and advance our conversations.

"Hi, Coach. How are you?" Robert's voice was upbeat.

"I am great Robert! I am busy but who isn't? How are you?"

Robert recounted the surface news of the last few weeks. We live on different coasts and each of us recounted the stages of weather we were experiencing and news about our families. Coaching is a bridge of trust that is relational. The more relational the approach, the greater the trust, and the more load the bridge can handle.

"I think I am at a good place," Robert continued. "I feel the impact of our last conversation because the load feels lighter. I have been more at peace with all that is occurring, and I know now that what lies ahead rests in His hands, and not mine."

"That is great man!" I responded. "You are not done Robert. I know you have much to contribute and many important years ahead. It feels like the more you return to that point of balance where you are able to be the 'true Robert', the better you'll feel and the more others will receive the help, insights and empowerment that you bring."

"I think I would like to explore the future and my next steps in our coaching conversation today. I think I might be ready to look more at how God might be disclosing what is ahead."

"As has been our pattern Robert, the agenda for our conversation is in your hands. Let's go for it."

We began to talk about Robert's current challenges within his organization and the needs of those he has been working with and seeking to resource. Coaching came to the forefront of our discussion. As I asked a series of questions, my goal was to help him explore and expand the topic so he was able to get all sides of his thinking out on the table. In particular, Robert was beginning to think about what it might look like to become more intentional in coaching others, and how he could make that a key component of his future.

"I have become a believer in coaching." Robert continued. "Helping others discover the answers they are searching for is an approach I wish I had used more of earlier in my leadership. Active listening, asking good questions and helping others pinpoint the issue holding them back are ways I can see that God wants me to continue to develop. Your coach training, Terry, and the tools you have developed are not only impactful in my life, but I believe they are key to my future."

Although I had seen Robert's excitement for coaching grow after he attended our training, these reflections were different. He was seeing a new way forward, and, most importantly, a way to offer to others the unique influence God had shaped him to have, that was not tied to a position. He could coach either within or without the bounds of an organizational position. I decided to verify the breakthrough he was potentially voicing.

"You are right, Robert. It really sounds like you have gained new clarity related to a possible future direction and a way you can offer yourself to others." I began. "How do you see all of this playing out? What could all of this mean?"

"I think this would mean I could offer coaching to the many leaders

I am encountering within the organization. We do well to provide information but are slow in seeing new behavior and transformation. A lot of our leaders are task-driven, and need the value of a coach to help them process all that they are encountering."

"Keep going Robert and play this out more for me." I replied.

"I can see possibly offering coach training to our leaders and embedding a coaching culture within our organization. It is what we need, and yet at this point it is foreign to much of how we operate. We are a 'telling' culture, and we need to be an 'asking' culture."

For the next several minutes, Robert expanded on both the value of coaching and the needs within the organization he served. As much as I love coaching, and would have loved to have taken the bait and talked all day on what coaching could mean for his organization, something more important was occurring. Robert was back to seeing himself only through the eyes of an organizational role, and not as one who has an influence to make regardless of his position.

"You know, friend, I could talk about this for the next couple of hours. But what would all this look like if you were not part of this organization in the future? What if you're suppose to launch 'Robert Grant Coaching,' and offer coaching to those within as well as the many outside the organization that you have relationships with all around the country?"

We had another one of those quiet moments. Robert had once again stopped dead in his tracks.

"Are you saying that I am not on the right track, and that I should not try to introduce coaching to our organization?" He replied. "It is something we talked about before and even have tried to implement in some of our meetings and resourcing times."

"No, that is not why I asked the question." I replied. "Why do you think I asked that?" I sat quietly as Robert pondered my response.

"May I give you a hand here friend, and offer a comment if you think it would be helpful?" I asked.

"Please do." he responded.

"I am sure not trying to throw water on the parade. I actually think you would be a great coach, and you are onto what God is doing. But I think your 'old friend' has risen up again, and has tried to get into the game. Your first response was to tie yourself back to the organization and your loyalty there. I am challenging you to think outside that box. The organization is changing and your position is coming to a close. I am both affirming your new direction forward, but also challenging you to consider that the delivery vehicle you want may not be the one you need. It is not disloyal for you to think about your life outside the organization. In fact, I think it may be the most healthy thing you can do."

It was obvious this had hit Robert like a ton of bricks. He was staggering to stay in the conversation and receive the words what were intended as help and love, but he felt like he had taken another blow to the ribs.

"I did it again didn't I?" He said quietly under his breath. "I once again tied my identity to the organization as opposed to my influenc regardless of the organization. I can't believe how deep this strain of virus goes."

We both just sat there for a minute. It felt like this was Robert's last hurdle. One of the most important shifts that comes with the Finishing Transition is fully embracing the truth that position is not a requirement for influence. Because it runs so deep in our culture, even if the truth is embraced as an ideology, it still remains hard to adopt it behaviorally. We had come upon positional and organizational loyalty's last vestige of control.

"I see it, Terry. And I agree. Whatever happens in the future, I need to start thinking and living outside the confines of the organization. I need to free myself to recognize that I can offer what God has entrusted to me, in this final segment of my journey, to the people and opportunities He brings along my path. I am not defined by where I serve or even by whom I serve with, but by whom I serve."

"You got it Robert. It is a Faith Challenge, freeing you to follow God to the places and the people He wants you to serve."

"Breakthrough!"

It took the rest of our time to process all that occurred. It was more than just another coaching conversation. This meeting was both about clarity related to Robert's future role as a coach and guide, and was also a time of faith challenge as God was assuring Robert that He could be trusted to lead and guide him into the future.

We closed our time in prayer.

In the months ahead, Robert and I had several more coaching conversations. We still do today. But this was the beginning of the next chapter. It was the end of the Finishing Transition and the beginning of the Convergence stage of his development. He has moved on from the organization he has served so faithfully, he coaches many faithful Christ-followers, and has recruited even more to attend our *Coach Certificate Training*.[25]

These accounts of his transition were not about coaching, though coaching has had a big impact on this chapter of Robert's story. These were conversations about navigating through important moments of Robert's journey so he could be set free to leave behind what God had entrusted, and not become sidetracked by the issues and obstacles that have caused many to stumble. Without the Finishing Transition there is often a struggle to finish.

THE ISSUES

1. The Finishing Transition is about new freedom. We bring closure to the past delivery methods, and say yes to new ways to offer the influence God has entrusted to each of us. New systems are needed for this stage of the journey. Becoming comfortable with past delivery vehicles (job, position, role, organization, life stage, etc.) can often hold one back from being able to use one's influence effectively in the future.

2. The Finishing Transition is not only about **what** we have to offer, but about **how** we will offer it. Both can be stumbled over by even the most gifted Christ-followers. **What** you offer defines the skills, insights and values you have been entrusted with by God to share with others. **How** you offer defines the best way for others to access that help. Whatever way is best, it is key to remember that people often want to know who you are, before they will be open to receive all you have.

3. The Finishing Transition closes with a Faith Challenge. Trust and a new level of faith will be required as you step into this next chapter. This challenge to your faith is undergirded by your new-found belief that it is God who is at work authoring your future, and it is His provision that will sustain this final stage of the journey.

WANT MORE?

Here is a link to Leader Breakthru's website that will take you further on topics covered in this chapter:

lbu.leaderbreakthru.com/products/the-100-day-plan

PART THREE

the applications

Beginning well is a momentary thing; finishing well is a lifelong thing.[26]

—RAVI ZACHARIAS

When we are securely rooted in personal intimacy with the source of life, it will be possible to remain flexible without being relativistic, convinced without being rigid, willing to confront without being offensive, gentle and forgiving without being soft, and true witnesses without being manipulative.[27]

—HENRI J.M. NOUWEN

WHAT'S AHEAD?

In Chapters 9-12 we will focus on interpreting the Finishing Transition in various settings and contexts—each of which can be helped by the presence of a coach. We will review the differences between how men and women often process the Finishing Transition, the differences people experience within three different contexts—vocational ministry, the marketplace and the home setting—and we will explore how someone who is in pre-retirement faces the many questions of the Finishing Transition as opposed to those who have already "retired."

9
men & women

*My only aim is to finish the race and complete
the task Jesus has given to me.*

—ACTS 20:24

*The way of Jesus cannot be imposed or mapped — it requires an active
participation in following Jesus as he leads us through sometimes
strange and unfamiliar territory.*[28]

—EUGENE PETERSON

I launch into this chapter with a bit of fear and trepidation.

As I coach or train others to coach, I am often asked if men and women process transitions differently. My answer is yes. I find both similarities and differences. My goal in these next few pages is not to put anyone in a box, stereotype their behaviors or categorize the genders in any particular way. So please forgive me when it appears I am getting close to that edge. Rather, I would like to share some of what I have gleaned as it relates to coaching men and women through transitions, and in particular, through the Finishing Transition. If you would grant me grace, I believe these few thoughts could be helpful.

— *Terry Walling*

SIMILARITIES

After thirty years of coaching both men and women, I find there are more similarities now than there were in earlier years. I find today there is a greater hunger, whether man or woman, for contribution. Each are wanting to know that their lives have counted. Similar questions surface about how God has shaped their lives to contribute, and how they can be used to empower others with the gifts and skills they possess.

Though the paths they take to the Finishing Transition are often very different, both men and women stand at the moments surrounding the Finishing Transition with similar questions:

"What's next?"

"What should I be doing at this stage?"

"How should I approach these next years?"

"How can I make a difference? And for whom?"

"Was I faithful to God and what He desired for my life?"

"Were the people God put in my life encouraged and helped?"

"Were the things He wanted me to do accomplished?"

"Did my life make any difference?"

"Is my life still making a difference?"

"How can I live so I will finish well?"

I have noticed a significant shift in recent years when it comes to issues of career and vocation. With more women gaining access to the higher levels of position both men and women are now often asking similar questions related to the best way to express their influence in their final chapter. Access to board positions, organizational discussions, marketplace positions and new ministry roles for both men and women have created more common ground for those I am coaching.

I notice both men and women are arriving today at the Finishing Transition with a shared passion and concern for people, as opposed to just the loss of a job. Both men and women want to see more than just a task accomplished. They seek to influence family, kids and grandkids, along with the poor, displaced, trafficked and forgotten. The pain of others and needs of the community now surfaces on both lists.

Both men and women are after issues of purpose, priorities and planning. Both want to know they will still contribute in this stage of their journey, and that what they offer is the fullest expression of who they are. Both are hungry for adventure and rest. Both are hoping that what they have could somehow help others do it better. And finally, both want to finish well and to explore ways to use their gifts, abilities and skills to help others in significant ways as they navigate the end-game.

There are also some significant differences.

MEN & THE FINISHING TRANSITION

Men tend to derive their identity from their work.

What they do, the title they hold, and the craft they have mastered are key ways men define who they are to others. When confronted with the Finishing Transition and the loss of a job or position, a significant struggle can begin. I often communicate to those I am coaching through times of transition that: *"adults don't transition into nothing very well."* Men especially feel the need to land on their feet and make sure that they "move into something." Early coaching conversations are often spent disentangling what a person offers (*their role*) from the jobs or positions that they have held (*their vocation*). The separating of *position* and *influence* requires time. The influence each of us has is often impacted by the position we hold. But influence that makes a Kingdom difference is sourced in who we are as people and Christ-followers. Many years spent in the vocational world often falsely convince a man that his position in life or in the organization he serves is what has given him his voice.

One of the biggest hurdles that surfaces during the Finishing Transition is a need for relational empowerment, as opposed to relying on position or vocation as the path to effectively empower others. In their younger years, men often enjoy the camaraderie of friends and relationships to transact help or resources. As time moves on, males often isolate themselves behind their accomplishments, and are driven to solve problems utilizing the power and position as opposed to relationships with those they do life and work with. This generalization has its exceptions, but on a whole it can be recognized in the lives of many men. Regardless of personality types or lifestyle, many men find their identity in solving problems or accomplishing tasks. The older one gets, the more this seems to be true.

This pattern can make it difficult for a man to return to relational empowerment. The return is key though, because today's millennials are looking for relationship first and foremost, before they will accept insights or expertise. Though the older generations offer much in terms of knowledge, skills and values, with little or no relational bridge it is difficult to transact the help that is often needed by the young.

Here are three practices I have used as I coach men who are confronting the issues surrounding the Finishing Transitions:

1. **Preview:** The concepts of Convergence and the reality of the Finishing Transition often need to be explained before men are willing to discuss their own experience. Men are used to cutting corners and getting to the point. For them to invest, it first needs to make sense. Often, they need to have God's purposes and the issues of Convergence explained, as well as what the outcomes will be before the coaching itself begins.

2. **Frequency:** The frequency and number of coaching conversations is often directly related to the depth of the conversations. The more conversations, the deeper the coaching often goes. It may not be until conversation three or four before the real obstacles and struggles come out on the table and the coach is trusted to be able to help.

3. **Different:** True coaching is different. Many men (especially those from the marketplace) hire and work with consultants or experts to fix problems and solve struggles. They can often view coaching with that lens. True coaching (drawing insights out verses putting them in) can often feel foreign, especially in the beginning. Coaching relationships within the workplace are often closer to mentoring relationships. When it comes to personal development, it may take time for a male leader or any Christ-follower to feel comfortable processing the uncertainty of a transition and issues of past development.

WOMEN & THE FINISHING TRANSITION

Much of what we discussed related to coaching men also applies to coaching women. And, much of what I will unpack when I talk about coaching women can also apply to men. But when I coach women who are facing the Finishing Transition they have unique needs. For one thing, women tend to see the issues behind the issues. They have an incredible ability to integrate factors quicker, and they bring the capacity to see multiple issues at once to our coaching conversations.

On a whole, women are often able to see the implications of decisions and breakdowns in problem-solving faster and with greater detail. They tend to also process information more deeply. They are looking for how factors work together for a clear direction forward, and are often concerned with what could circumvent one's future direction. Many women are practical strategists because they look at all sides of the issues. It is key to make sure many of these assets are employed as they are coached through the Finishing Transition. They can often already see the pitfalls and obstacles, as well as a potential path forward.

Women tend to be better at blending their life and needs around the circumstances of others. This is accelerated if they are married and/or raising children. Their life has had to fit around their family and others. Career women who are married and have children have felt this all the more. On a whole, it makes them more collaborative than men. They often see themselves as part of a system, and therefore what they can do in the future is often cast on the backdrop of others. Seeing the needs of the many and surrendering one's own needs is biblical and strikes at the very core of servanthood. But one's identity in Christ should not be the casualty of a servanthood posture.

The biggest hurdle I have encountered in helping women in transition as a whole, and with those who are navigating the Finishing Transition in particular, is that they need to give themselves permission to think according to who they are, and what they offer to others. Woman often feel they need permission to think about themself and their needs. Systems and organizations around her have placed expectations and restraints on how far her dreams can take her. For many women, they have spent much of their life surrendering plans and dreams to the agendas and demands of others. Often, they lose themselves, or believe their contribution is not valued. Many times my coaching conversations have sought to surface what God has entrusted to them, and help them become convinced that others need what they offer, regardless of the struggle it may take to share it.

Each of us, man or woman, have been created to do good deeds. These good deeds have bee authored by God Himself before time began (Ephesians 2:10). A woman's discovery of her unique contribution, and the living into this contribution in this third stage of her development often entails a series of core components as she confronts the Finishing Transition.

Here are three helps:

1. **Focus**: Typically, women come to coaching with an interwoven fabric of issues that first need to be disentangled, and then regrouped together in a series of issue-oriented file folders. Once clarified, she can now bring focus to what needs to be addressed, and what can wait. Once the decks are cleared, she is better able to go after what is most important and gain focus.

2. **Unique:** Many of the issues and dreams that surface in the Finishing Transition have been on the back burner for a long time, to the point that she feels that what she has to offer is commonplace and not worthy of all this attention. Often times, coaching in this stage is spent convincing and embracing how the unique set of gifts and experiences produce a valued contribution that others need.

3. **Collaborative:** Because of the places where they find themselves—the dominance of males and the reality that everything is related—women tend to be more collaborative in their approach. While this is good when it comes to team building, it can hold them back when it comes to clarifying unique contribution. They often find themselves needing to "check off" what others see and think. A coach can offer this sense of collaboration while helping to better define what she has to give to others.

WANT MORE?

Here is a link to Leader Breakthru's website that will take you further on topics covered in this chapter:

www.leaderbreakthru.com/stuck-the-book

10

ministry, marketplace, & the home

We are all faced with a series of great opportunities brilliantly disguised as impossible situations.[29]
—CHUCK SWINDOLL

The homemaker has the ultimate career. All other careers exist for one purpose only—and that is to support the ultimate career.[30]
—C.S. LEWIS

It is often hard to get Christians to see that God is willing not just to use men and women in ministry, but in law, in medicine, in business, in the arts. This is the great shortfall today.[31]
—DICK LUCAS

Whether in vocational ministry, serving in the marketplace setting, or at home raising kings and queens for the Kingdom, each context presents challenges and questions from the eye of the "Finishing Transition storm". Each of us will confront the reality of transitions. Having coached believers from all three settings, I have found passionate Christ-followers who desire to see their lives count. In this chapter we offer insights and helps for each setting.

VOCATIONAL MINISTRY

Those who enter the Finishing Transition from the viewpoint of vocational ministry, have a journey similar to the one Robert Grant shared in the early chapters of this book. Robert comes from the world of mission and ministry, and expresses many of the challenges of those who have invested much of their lives and experience on caring for the Church, and advancing the cause of Christ.

Those in the vocational ministry sector have become accustomed to people in need coming to them. Whether in the local church or mission ministry, the day-to-day is often constant and the phone never stops ringing. One of the biggest challenges comes when those in need stop calling and the demanding schedule ceases. Many begin to feel a sense of loss and of not being needed.

The empty schedule is often further matched by the loss of people seeking them out for advice and counsel as well as the fulfillment that comes through solving the needs of others. It would not be uncommon for a minister or mission leader to experience feelings of depression and low motivation. Many feel lost in terms of how to spend their time. The Finishing Transition initiates a time to rethink one's purpose and the use of one's gifts.

Jobs, positions or past assignments are delivery systems for influence. What needs to be re-thought is what a new delivery system could be, and if there should be multiple delivery systems? Leaders often find that they need more than one way to express the influence God has shaped them to make. Here are four tips for those in the vocational ministry setting and who are moving through the Finishing Transition and into Convergence.

Tip #1: Break free from extreme loyalty.

Though you may have served one tribe or group during your time in ministry, begin to see yourself ministering in other worlds. It is not betrayal to move on.

Tip #2: Break free from the stage.

Though much of your time may have been in a "center stage" place of authority and communication, getting off the stage allows you to have a more effective ministry posture as someone who is supportive and is of little threat to the system.

Tip #3: Break free from the stereotype (chaplain).

Many people who have exited pastoral ministry become a mainstay for pastoral care and preaching. You must resist seeing yourself as someone who is only qualified as a pulpit fill-in or as an older-person chaplain.

Tip #4: Break free from self-promotion.

A desire to offer what one has to give often causes an individual to move into the world of self-promotion or social media. But most people would like to know how to relate to you and how to access what you offer. Also remember that when in full-time ministry, most of the needs and individuals come to you. In this next stage, you must offer the help to others.

MARKETPLACE / WORKPLACE

For many years, those in the marketplace have been consumed by the demands of work or of running a business. They often have little time to give attention and focus to what life looks like after the demands of work cease. While the ministry sector has learned to rely upon their giving, the marketplace individual often begins to feel that their finances are the "primary" way to support Kingdom ministry. But the skills, abilities, and experiences a marketplace individual can offer, bring Kingdom influence to many. One of the core purposes of the Finishing Transition is to break the belief that communicates I have little to offer in terms of ministry. What a marketplace individual needs is clarity related to what they offer and the contribution they make, besides just their money. New focus and intentionality are key ways to move beyond these early obstacles in thinking.

Here are four tips for those who find themselves in the marketplace setting and who are moving through the Finishing Transition and into Convergence.

Tip #1: Break free from seeing yourself as different.

The separation of "clergy-laity" has been so ingrained and played out each Sunday that it often creates a second-class system in the Church that was not intended nor seen in scripture. A marketplace Christ-follower is often more impactful because they are not caught in the trap of "playing church." Choose to see yourself as a believer in Christ with gifts and a set of experiences that have been given by Christ for ministry.

Tip #2: Break free from local only.

Think beyond local. What you offer could be needed regionally and across the landscape of organizations and geography. As you clarify your contribution and as you begin to think through where/who you might help, consider serving locally but also have an openness to serve globally. Your past business contacts could open the door to think beyond your back door.

Tip #3: Break free from problem-solving alone.

Possessing some of the insights you have and knowing what you know may open the door for you to serve and minister to needs. Don't pigeon-hole yourself as if that is all you offer. You may have discernment gifts, exhortative gifts, prophetic gifts, a call to prayer and healing or to biblical teaching. Like those in vocational ministry, begin to recognize that the felt need is often the opening of a door to the real need.

Tip #4: Break free from needing to rest.

While you may be entering into the Finishing Transition out-of-gas and in need of a break, don't stay there. Many who have entered this stage from the marketplace setting have said that the question that quickly arises is "What am I going to do?" Grant yourself both the freedom to live in new ways, yet to recognize the value that comes with new assignments and redefined rhythms of work.

HOMEMAKERS

Most who enter into the Finishing Transition through the homemaker path have often focused their attention on caring for the day-to-day needs of their home, their families, and those they feel called to nurture. For much of their lives, they have seen the home as their main place of influence, regardless if they worked outside the home. At times, those who serve at home, rate the skills and experiences they use in the home setting as commonplace—ones that most people possess. They tend minimize what it takes to organize schedules, feed and care for their loved ones, navigate and work with different personality types, and adjust to the constant changes and emergencies of daily life, but this is no small feat. Homemakers possess many of the same skills required to run a small business. Both roles involve people management, counseling and handling conflicts, managing and accomplishing key projects, caring for daily operations, problem-solving, crisis intervention, bookkeeping and money management, and more. On top of all of this, those who influence others in the home are often taken for granted and can lose touch with who they are as they serve the needs of others. When the seasons of life change, and many of the duties at home shift as family comes and goes, those at home can begin to feel a lack of value as they find themselves with fewer things to do in the home and no ideas of what they could do outside the home.

The Finishing Transition for homemakers is often about learning to value what they have to offer, and repurposing what they offer as new expressions of their skills and experiences God has used to served others. It is not that their family no longer needs them, but they often need them in new ways. And it is not that those in the home have little value in the workplace or ministry setting, but they need to learn how to translate their gifts and experiences into new situations. Often this requires the rebuilding of confidence and reassurance that others need and desire what they have to offer. Some of these individuals who have been serving as homemakers made conscious decisions earlier to step back from the career track into order to be at home. Their absence from the workplace can bring on doubts in their abilities and skills as they seek to reenter influence outside the home.

Here are four tips for those who find themselves in the homemaking setting and who are moving through the Finishing Transition and onto Convergence.

Tip #1: Don't discount. Believe those you trust.

Though you may feel like people are just trying to help you cope with the "empty nest" and its challenges, pick a few voices that you trust, and ask them for help in translating you and your skills beyond the home front. And then when they give you advice or help, believe them. Let them be your springboard to face the future in new ways.

Tip #2: Take baby steps.

It becomes easier as you take each step. And as you step out, God continues to unfold what He is doing, and how He wants to use you in the future. Sometimes you can't think your way into a change. We often must behave our way into the future.

Tip #3: Give yourself grace.

You will try and fail. Give yourself grace and each new step will add new insights and additional ways to see how you contribute best. New settings will help you learn.

Tip #4: Seek a coach to help.

Choosing to see yourself in a new way is not a betrayal to your family or their needs. It is close to impossible to navigate this change alone. Find another person to walk with you during this time who can help move you past the transition and into Convergence.

A final note:

Home is one of several major bases of influence. Convergence is about making your unique and ultimate contribution whether at home, in the marketplace or in a mission setting. God uses the home as an important domain of influence where values, attitudes and self-esteem is shaped. A Christ-follower's role there, whether female or male, offers ways to form and mentor leaders and passionate Christ-followers.

WANT MORE?

Here is a link to Leader Breakthru's website that will take you further on topics covered in this chapter:

lbu.leaderbreakthru.com/products/transformation-paradoxes

11

finishing: pre-retirement

"We feel lost when it comes to how this retirement thing is supposed to work. Can you help?"

"We've been thinking a lot about this time of our lives, and all of sudden we feel the impact of the questions on how to do this right."

"We see a lot of examples of how to not do retirement well. How do we navigate all this, especially in light of our commitment to Christ?"

"We've planned a lot of travel and time to do what we never have gotten to do because of kids and life. Is that wrong?"

Most individuals contemplate the issues surrounding the Finishing Transition and the end-game before they step away from employment. The launch of this transition surfaces more questions than answers. Some hold off on planning, believing they have many years left before needing to think about the "end-game." But then the Finishing Transition arrives often sooner than they think and unannounced. There are several factors that can help to embrace the Finishing Transition, whether one is ready or still sits on this side of full-time employment. They include:

1. Changes often come within the company, organization or ministry—downsizing personnel, financial down-turns, management turnover, and/or a desire for younger leadership. This can result in the loss of position and serve as an Entry moment into the transition.

2. A restlessness that prompts a Christ-follower to plan their end-game—wanting to be well prepared for the days ahead and wanting their remaining years to be productive. This could even include a focus on mission and ministry.

3. Changes related to life, health and the choices of others. A Christ-follower encounters life changes they did not anticipate which throw life into a time of uncertainty and chaos. Though they are not ready for a different life, it has arrived on their doorstep.

Christ-followers who are in the pre-retirement stage are often looking for information and answers and caught off guard by the Finishing Transition. Right in the middle of trying to cope with the demands of life and work, there is upheaval in their spiritual journey. Questions related to life direction, purpose, fulfillment, uncertainty, isolation, confusion and fear all appear out of nowhere. It is possible to not recognize the Finishing Transition when it surfaces with its many questions related to what's next.

In Chapter 3 we reviewed how the culture's view of this time has taken on a fixed-age and fixed-mindset—that years after 66 should be seen and experienced differently than the years before. This same mindset has been adopted by the Church—denominations, mission agencies, local churches, and every-day believers. The Church has embraced the assumption that when you are done with employment your are done contributing, and it is time to rest.

Does energy and capacity lessen as you get older? You bet.

Do organizations need influx of new ideas and creativity from the younger generations. Of course.

Do one's desires in life change, and do individuals want different things at the end? Yes!

And, does the end-game present new challenges by way of health, family, work and finances? Yes! It's obvious that life at the end is a unique season.

With all that said, these changes never add up to suspending life, work and ministry. They do not mean that one should hold back on their unique contribution which God has been crafting over their lifetime.

PRE-RETIREMENT & THE FINISHING TRANSITION

For these individuals there is an urgency to better understand the end-game, and how to navigate the pressures they are beginning to feel. The Finishing Transition brings key questions to the surface that will serve to propel them into the next chapter of their life and personal development. With these questions comes the need for new paradigms and new ways of thinking through what lies ahead.

There are multiple facets that need to be explored related to retirement—finances, housing, health concerns and emotional wholeness just to name a few. Issues of purpose and focus often surface as basic needs and plans for retirement are confirmed. Options and opportunities for involvement also begin to surface as a result of the lack of vocational commitments. Before long-term commitments are made, it is helpful to take a step back and ask three important questions:

What? What do I have that I can offer to others? (contribution)

How? How can I best exchange my "what" with others? (delivery methods)

Why? Why do I want to invest what I have in others (purpose)

These three questions can be arranged in three, concentric circles, working from the inside-out; Why? How? What?

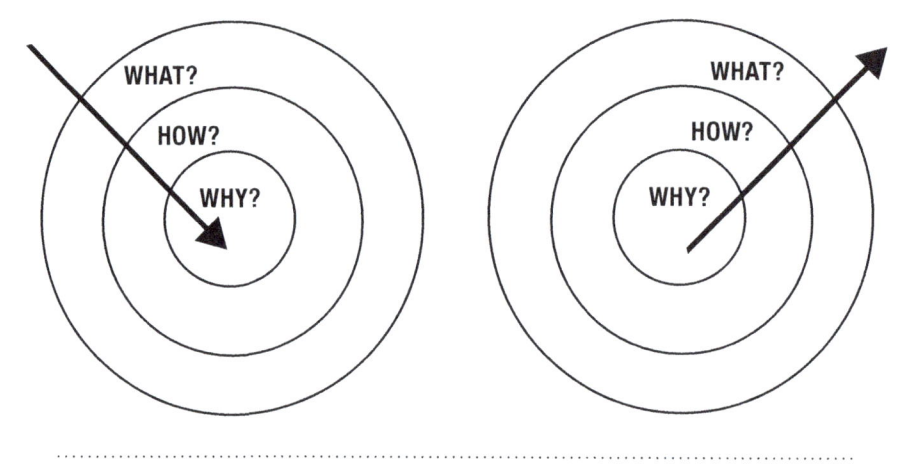

```
        The Cultural Approach                    The Kingdom Approach
```

The arrow that moves from the outside to the inside depicts the typical cultural approach to life—our identity is based around what I have and the expertise I think they want. It is a life that has been based on performance and external value. When the direction of the arrow moves from the inside to the outside, it depicts a more Kingdom approach to life—knowing that our identity and value rests in our relationship with Christ and who He says that we are. We offer ourselves, first and foremost, and then the knowledge and experience God has entrusted to each of us. Let's take a look at each of these questions more closely.

The question of **what** is focused on an individual's Major Role. Major Role is a concise definition of one's influence. It is more than one's job or vocation. Rather, it is a one-sentence summation of the contribution a Christ-follower brings to any person, environment or venue in which they find themselves. Clarifying one's role offers a decision-making grid to help a Christ-follower decide which option or opportunity fits best.

EXAMPLES OF MAJOR ROLE STATEMENTS:

- I seek to come alongside those I believe in, offer a relationship that surfaces insights they thought they did not have, and answers they know can only come with the help of Christ.

- I help others make their life *work*, whether to clarify a goal, solve a problem, or be able to better get from point "A" to point "B."

- I resource and coach breakthrough in the lives of risk-taking, Kingdom leaders, helping them move forward to make their unique contribution to the lives of others. (Note: This third one is my personal Major Role Statement, and is my decision-making grid for the individuals and situations I invest in.)

How? This question addresses the **delivery** of what God has entrusted to an individual, to the people who would benefit from it. Delivery systems, or Core Methods, are the ways in which we live out our Major Role. They could also be described as the core functions we have learned to do. They can be formal or informal, tasks or relationships, recognized or unrecognized, done as a professional or as a volunteer. The point is knowing the way others access one's resources, and the ways that they are helped by your presence and involvement. If you do not know what you offer, and how to offer it, it is often hard for others to access what you have. Some employ multiple ways to deliver what they offer.

Examples of **how** to deliver one's Major Role:

1. As a teacher-mentor on a church's staff
2. As a Personal Development Life Coach
3. As a *Moms-in-Touch* group leader

Why? This question speaks to issues of motives and purpose. The why should never be assumed. The *why* must be revisited. In the endgame, it is often the *why* that helps push an individual beyond being dismissed and passed over. The driving force of the Christ-follower is not personal mission but rather Kingdom advance. Those focused on making their Kingdom contribution at the end, live and serve out of a motive of worship—loving God with all their mind, body and soul.

finishing

They seek to express a passion for Christ sourced from the years of relationship with and faithfulness of their God by being the person He has created them to be.

Examples of *why* statements:

- Because I found life, when I met Christ, I now seek to offer what I have to others, just as He offered life, hope and help to me.
- My passion is to be the Church, not just attend church. I can best offer who I am, first and foremost, before I offer what I think I have.
- All of life is because of Christ. Therefore at the end, I once again affirm and offer back all of my life.

Some questions to reflect on as you face decisions related to retirement:

1. What Has God been saying and doing lately related to the end-game, and your purposes for this stage of your journey?

2. If you were to ask others, what would they say has been the significant role you have played in their life or ministry?

3. When you think about what you offer to others, how do you sense that God has used you in other's lives through the years?

WANT MORE?

Here is a link to Leader Breakthru's website that will take you further on topics covered in this chapter:

www.leaderbreakthru.com/convergence

12

finishing: post-retirement

"We are busier now than before we retired. Crazy!

We never envisioned it being like this"

*"You can only go to so many places, and do so many trips.
I'm bored. I've got to do something."*

*"We are having a hard time sorting all this out and knowing how much time to
give to the church, to our kids and to the things we want to do."*

"Don't we deserve to rest? It's time for the younger generation to take over.

Besides, they don't want us just hanging around, right?"

The Finishing Transition sometimes waits until an individual has entered retirement life. Disillusionment and lack of focus can often promote the launch of the transition. Those who have "retired" often are more exhausted than before their retirement. Many people who are in this situation are surprised by how busy life has become and how consumed they have becomes with the needs and the distractions of life. It is not uncommon to become frustrated and disillusioned about what they thought would be an enjoyable time in life.

Factors that can launch the Finishing Transition for those who have retired or who have already stepped away from employment often include:

1. Busyness and competing agendas. These can begin to usher in a time of exhaustion, questioning and even disillusionment. What once was something that an individual looked forward to has now become something they seek to escape.

2. The earlier dreams of retirement seem to be slipping away. What once was an exciting, driving force no longer seems possible, or even a potential. Changes and fears around security have begun to crowd out what once was desired and thought to be possible.

3. Changing needs of family and friends. Though family is of highest importance, caring for the needs of family members begins to close the door on time, options and energy. The needs of parents, kids, grandkids or close friends can move into the space once reserved for "retirement plans" and once again, duty and responsibility become the priority.

Earlier we discussed the evolution of the retirement period. Retirement is an invention of culture and there is no biblical foundations. The Finishing Transition seeks to initiate clarity of one's ultimate contribution. In pre-retirement transitions, God initiates clarity and direction for pending decisions. In post-retirement transitions God seeks to bring clarity to confusion that has often arisen as a result of retirement.

Those in post-retirement should consider the following four questions as a way to help them sort out what is occurring, and how best to move forward:

What's Right?

What is occurring that is in line with the contribution God has called you to make, and needs to be enhanced and done more frequently?

What's Wrong?

What is occurring that is not part of how God has shaped you to contribute, and is consuming too much time, energy and focus?

What's Missing?

What is not a part of your current involvement and expression that needs to be added? Often there are new (and different) ways to express your contribution that need to be explored.

What's Confused?

What is occurring that needs greater clarity or definition, and needs to be considered as a possible way to deliver your influence in the future?

Answers to these four questions offer ways to sort through your current situation, and help an individual to address the three questions (What? How? Why?) that are discussed previously under "pre-retirement."

THE POINT OF RETIREMENT

After spending so much time on the logistics of retiring, it's easy to lose sight of the bigger picture. Is financial security your real goal, or is there an ultimate purpose and contribution that lies beyond the dollars or place to reside? In other words, what have you retired to? Reluctance to tackle the bigger questions can often hold back individuals as they are swept up in the growing busyness of retired life. Clarifying (or re-clarifying) your purpose at the third stage of the journey is often essential, and helps to bring meaning back to the surprise of a busy life.

At its simplest, *meaning* can be defined as being connected to something larger than one's self. It can mean participating on a sports team, belonging to an organization, or serving an important cause. For Christ-followers, meaning is often defined as knowing that one's final chapter in life counts towards Kingdom purposes. Knowing one's "purpose" is no longer about holding a title or position, but about knowing that life is being spent on the right things, and with the right people.

The Church of Scotland at Edinburgh in 1648 approved its shorter version of the Westminster Catechism by offering an answer to one of life's most critical questions: What is the chief aim (end) of man? In other words: What is the purpose of life? Their answer is deeply profound for its summation and simplicity. *Man's chief end is to glorify God, and to enjoy him for ever.* Out of that purpose flows a life of meaning.

Purpose has two major components—the call to *be* and the call to *do*. The call to **be** has to do with choosing to grow deeper in one's journey with God, and experiencing ongoing self-awareness. The call to **do** has to do with contributing to people, to a cause or performing a core function. Meaning sometimes becomes the goal and desire of many, but clarity in one's purpose provides the well from which true meaning is drawn.

What is your statement of purpose, for this third chapter of your journey and for your life overall? Here are some examples:

> *My purpose is to grow deeper in my love for God as I seek to empower my family and close friends with a meaning for life that will transcend their days.*

> *My purpose at the end is to live like it was the beginning—with a childlike faith and a trust in God that will do what He asks and share all that I have with others.*

> *My purpose comes out of all the God has shown me related to how business can be an onramp to ministry. I want to mentor, coach and disciple those in the marketplace to see their skills and venue as a unique mission field.*

> *My bucket list will never be completed here. My passion is prayer, deeper intimacy and intercession that will release an epic, new work of God, far beyond my life.*

Some additional thoughts for those experience the Finishing Transition in the post-retirement days:

Encore—Retirement is a time to stop working at tasks that do not express your unique contribution or are simply to earn money. Purpose during retirement is more than just doing multiple tasks and responding to the many needs. It is an opportunity to launch a focused endeavor or even a small business, whose purpose is not income alone. Taking big risks and betting on unproven ideas should be left to others at this stage, but focusing time and energy on something unique to you that addresses a need in our world and extends Christ Kingdom, should not be ruled out.

Giving Back—Gratitude is the gateway spiritual discipline. Giving back could mean volunteering in a passion area, teaching and sharing your knowledge, or serving on a business or organizational board. The key is involvement in something that you have a passion to see strengthened, and which would benefit others for Christ. The focus is not about simply giving funds, but involving yourself and investing in something that matters.

Spiritual Growth—During the working years, during the years of child-raising, throughout the frenetic pace of life, our spiritual, interior growth often falls into the "important-but-not-urgent" basket. For some, these years of life need to be a time of reimmersing themselves into spiritual community. It can also mean traveling down a fresh spiritual path—freed from earlier constraints. Fueling a greater work of God can offer purpose to retirement and equip a Christ-follower to offer new gifts to others.

Am I "wasting" my final days?"

It is a question that can creep into the minds and hearts of those living out their final days. The answer to that question is often addressed as one clarifies purpose.

What about you? What is, or needs to be, your purpose now that you are no longer consumed by going to work, a paycheck or your duty and responsibility to others?

> **WANT MORE?**
>
> Here is a link to Leader Breakthru's website that will take you further on topics covered in this chapter:
>
> **www.leaderbreakthru.com/convergence**

PART FOUR

the helps

The Christian experience, from start to finish, is a journey of faith.[32]

—WATCHMAN NEE

We need to discover all over again that worship is natural to the Christian, as it was to the godly Israelites who wrote the psalms, and that the habit of celebrating the greatness and graciousness of God yields an endless flow of thankfulness, joy, and zeal.[33]

—J.I. PACKER

WHAT'S AHEAD?

In Chapters 13-15 we will offer resources and tools to help you process the Finishing Transition.

In Chapter 13 we will identify four ways to approach this stage.

In Chapter 14 we will introduce exercises that can be used to process through the issues that surface during this transition.

In Chapter 15 we will provide an overview of personal development coaching as well as one of Leader Breakthru's online learning processes—*Resonance*.

13

four postures

The terrible thing, the almost impossible thing, is to hand over your whole self— all your wishes and precautions—to Christ.[34]
—C.S. LEWIS

Attitudes determine our actions, for good or bad.[35]
—DWIGHT L. MOODY

Psalm 90 was written near the end of Moses' life. As he took a look back, Moses reflected on just how short life really was, especially when viewed from God's eternal vantage point. A paraphrase of verse 12 reads, *"Teach us to wisely apply ourselves so that our lives count."* In verse 17, Moses' heart cry was for people to live their lives out of a desire to finish well, *"May the favor[a] of the Lord our God rest on us; establish the work of our hands for us—yes, establish the work of our hands."* The final days also involve the work of our hands.

Up to this point, our skills and natural abilities have mastered the challenges we have faced. But now things are changing. When we were younger, stronger, and quicker to adopt the new ideas, answers came over time. But now, life is numbered by days.

Is it possible for a business leader to have the same influence on others now that he or she has stepped aside from their role and no longer frequents the office, or interacts with the day-to-day?

Is it possible for a mother, who has served those close to her so faithfully, to still be able to influence her family and others around her, even though she now finds herself in an empty nest and doesn't have as much contact with those closest to her?

Is it possible for those who have served in vocational ministry roles to still have a voice in the Church and in the hearts and lives of those they no longer lead through their position?

These answers often depend on the attitude and approach one takes to this new stage in their development. Whether in the marketplace, ministry or home settings, all of life's experiences are being woven together by God to yield an ultimate, Kingdom contribution.

The Four Postures provide one way to measure our readiness to enter into this next stage of development and to live a life that counts and finish well. When we take a look at the lives of those who did finish well, there are four postures that stand out. It is helpful for Christ-followers to measure their current behavior and attitudes using these four postures.

THE FOUR POSTURES

1. Modeling—Living out the truth you believe in. This involves issues of authenticity, lifelong learning and openness.

2. Relating—Relationally valuing those whom God gives you a desire to help/influence. This involves issues of trust, the importance of asking rather than telling and the importance of offering one's self before you offer answers.

3. Exchanging—Turning your resources into resources for others. This involves issues of stewardship, faithfulness and trusting others.

4. Entrusting—Giving to others what has been entrusted to you by God. This involves issues of generosity, discernment and intentionality.

Posture 1: Modeling

While the title of "modeling," may not be your first choice, its listed first because of its high importance within the context of Convergence. Modeling speaks to issues of authenticity and genuineness. In the end, the soil of true impact on others must be replete with the nutrients of what's "real." People around us are listening to our life more than our words. Spiritual authority is entrusted to those in the endgame who choose to continue to live out their faith and love of Christ. The key to this posture is trusting in Who you know—Christ— rather than in what you know.

Modeling the Christian life is not done as an outward display but rather as a way to show others how inward convictions are translated into outward behavior. It involves the integrity of living out the Christlike life. The translation of one's faith into outward action is often sorely lacking, and should not be underestimated.

We see Daniel choose to live out his faith as a young man and make choices that resulted in the Lord's protection in a lion's den and presence in his life. We see Joshua choose to stay true to his faith and to live according to what was true, no matter how many turned and walked away from it.

> "Now fear the Lord and serve him with all faithfulness. Throw away the gods your ancestors worshiped beyond the Euphrates River and in Egypt, and serve the Lord. But if serving the Lord seems undesirable to you, then choose for yourselves this day whom you will

serve, whether the gods your ancestors served beyond the Euphrates, or the gods of the Amorites, in whose land you are living. But as for me and my household, we will serve the Lord." —Joshua 24:14-15

Adopting the posture of modeling often involves three mindsets, each creating an openness to God and others that serves to invite a time of Convergence.

1. **Be accessible**: Place yourself in a posture of engagement with others, their ideas and their input. If others know there is a bridge built between you and them, they are more likely to use it. As you choose to be open to God and His continuing work in your life, His work within you attracts others who want to grow.

2. **Life-long learning**: Placing yourself in a posture of growth and as a learner, helps to creates the potential for dialogue and exchange. As you continue to grow your walk with God, you are better able to translate life to others.

3. **Display openness:** Place yourself in a posture of willingness to reexamine the issues of the faith. This gives you an opportunity to support, rather than be seen as unapproachable.

Posture 2: Relating

Regardless of whether one is an introvert or an extrovert, the endgame involves much more than tasks—it's about relational engagement with others and the sharing one's resources. The posture of relating involves the ability to express interest in another, their world and their needs. It means entering into someone else's world. The younger generations desire relationship first and foremost, before they will care about the answers one offers. You may think you have little to offer just by being yourself. But who you are as a person, may be the greatest gift and need for the person on the other side of the table. If they can know who you are, then they can learn to trust your insights in greater ways.

Many people you come across may be going into battle for the first time—going after goals and facing obstacles that they may feel are insurmountable. Like young Jonathan's stand with David, and an older leader like Barnabas who stood by a young John-Mark in the Scriptures, building the capacity to relate and trust one another is the seedbed of breakthrough.

> "When Barnabas and Saul had finished their mission, they returned from Jerusalem, taking with them John, also called Mark."
> —Acts 12:25

Adopting the posture of relating also involves three mindsets, each requiring time and involvement, and each tilling the soil of Convergence.

1. **The person is more important than the problem:** Helping, resourcing and coaching is about the person first and foremost. God often uses the problem to get back to the person. Caring first for the person creates the potential for a deeper exploration of the real problem.

2. **It is more important to ask than to tell:** Wanting to know what they think before making sure they know what you think helps promote discovery and greatest ownership of the problem on their part.

3. **The relationship is as important as the answers:** Most people today have been targeted, marketed, tricked and have become weary of the next popular approach. A genuine offer of friendship may at first create suspicion. As time moves forward however, and friendship becomes the goal, new avenues of help and exchange will open up.

Posture 3: Exchanging

To exchange is to cultivate a posture of generosity—knowing that one cannot keep that which one has never owned. While there are many needs that surround issues of mission and ministry, exchanging is about matching resources with corresponding needs, whether that exchange involves tangible or intangible resources.

Exchanging cultivates a posture of giving. The mindset shifts to helping others be successful as opposed to amassing resources for the future. At times, the withholding of resources is prudent and needed, but the exchanging of resources is critical in this new stage of one's development and creates opportunity for growth and Kingdom expansion.

Exchanging is also about stewardship. That which is known, gained and owned has been entrusted to be stewarded. The ability to steward relates to goals and mission. Entrusted to each of us are a set of experiences, insights and goods to help extend Christ's Kingdom.

The exchange and sharing of resources was a hallmark of Joseph's life as he dispensed help to the brothers who had sold him into slavery. His desire was not to hold, prove or exact retribution. Instead, his approach was to recognize the greater work of God and to bring life to many.

> "His brothers then came and threw themselves down before him. 'We are your slaves,' they said. But Joseph said to them, 'Don't be afraid. Am I in the place of God? You intended to harm me, but God intended it for good to accomplish what is now being done, the saving of many lives. So then, don't be afraid. I will provide for you and your children.' And he reassured them and spoke kindly to them."
> —Genesis 50:18-21

Adopting the posture of exchanging is facilitated by three mindsets that each foster the importance of giving to others, and create a posture of open-handedness.

1. **Stewardship**: Stewardship means that you can recognize that what you have been entrusted with is meant to serve a greater purpose than simply self-preservation.

2. **Faithfulness**: Being faithful requires that you recognize that much will be required from those who are given much. Those who have been given resources and opportunities need to faithfully dispense them to others.

3. **Trust**: Those who place their trust in God become trustworthy. God's provision and faithfulness is often the by-product of trusting in Him rather than turning to one's own logic or abilities. Our deeper trust in God yields increased authority and power to influence others.

Posture 4: Entrusting

While exchanging is about releasing what you've been holding onto, entrusting goes further and seeks to know that resources are placed in the hands of those who will steward them well. While there are never guarantees, entrusting our resources to others allows them to go beyond our limitations.

Entrusting resources is often more about supporting the person rather than supporting new initiatives or ideas. While it's the people who drive ideas and projects, it is the character of the individual or the organization that should be the baseline consideration when it comes to the entrustment of resources. In the end, it will be the motives and the mission of those we seek to serve that will direct the use of the resources you are entrusting. The entrusting of resources is seen in Paul's collection of the offering for the Church in Jerusalem, and in the negative withholding of Ananias and Sapphira during the early church movement:

> *"Ananias, how is it that Satan has so filled your heart that you have lied to the Holy Spirit and have kept for yourself some of the money you received for the land? Didn't it belong to you before it was sold? And after it was sold, wasn't the money at your disposal? What made you think of doing such a thing? You have not lied just to human beings but to God." —Acts 5:3-4*

Adopting the posture of entrusting is facilitated by the application of three mindsets that help guide the dispensing of one's resources to others.

1. **Transparency**: Open dialogue and exchange with the persons involved is as important as a commitment to a need or mission. This creates relationship and ownership of the process by those who give and those who receive.

2. **Discernment**: Entrusting is a spiritual process, with prayer and guidance from the Holy Spirit involved in the disbursement of resources.

3. **Focus**: Matching purpose with needs is essential. Needs will vary, but we can look for a connection between our unique contribution and the needs of others.

These four postures (Modeling, Relating, Exchanging, Entrusting) create an environment and an attitude that help increase the potential for Kingdom advancement during the Convergence stage in one's development. These postures provide tangible attitudes that can be cultivated. But what more can be done to match one's desire to serve with the many needs of our world?

Keep reading.

WANT MORE?

Here is a link to Leader Breakthru's website that will take you further on topics covered in this chapter:

lbu.leaderbreakthru.com/products/understanding-mentoring

14

three constructs

I have held many things in my hands, and I have lost them all; but whatever I have placed in God's hands, that, I still possess.
—MARTIN LUTHER

Do not be anxious about anything, but in every situation, by prayer and petition, with thanksgiving, present your requests to God.
—PHILIPPIANS 4:6

Constructs are exercises that use models and paradigms to help clarify one's thinking. Transitions are often about processing one's thinking and consolidating one's lessons from the past to help guide the future. The Finishing Transition seeks to bring summation to one's life experiences that chart the course towards Convergence. There are three constructs, or exercises, that can help one cultivate greater understanding of what God has entrusted to a Christ-follower that can be shared with others:

1. Five Words
2. Five Circles
3. Thirteen Ways

FIVE WORDS

This exercise seeks to summarize the essence of one's unique and ultimate contribution into five words. Oftentimes, reflection exercises focus on wordsmith statements that sound impressive, all the while losing the essence of what a person is seeking to distill. In the Five Words Construct, we are after five, core words that identify the essence of your contribution.

Each word serves as a capstone that encompasses how your behavior or attributes influence those God sends your way. They describe the contribution you make to a team, organization, ministry or project.

The Five Words are not all encompassing, but rather they begin to express a Christ-follower's unique contribution. Each word may not feel unique in itself, but when all five words are wedded together, their combination describes a unique expression.

The Five Words Exercise

Brainstorm: List as many words as you can that describe how you contribute to others. Make sure to think along the two-tracks—being and doing. Look for words that best describe:

1. **Who you are**—What are your values? Passions? Etc.?
2. **What you offer to others**—What is your contribution? Your skills? Talents? Innate gifts? Etc.?

Allow yourself the freedom to think outside of your current situation or position. Ask others for input.

Some examples of words you could choose would be: problem-solver, encourager, organizer, strategic, prophetic, honoring, faith, courage, hope, breakthrough, challenger, etc.

List between 10-20 words and then begin to distill them into five words that describe the essentials of what you offer to others. Next to each word, provide a definition that helps to better articulate what that word represents. For example:

- **Catalyst:** I seek to help others see the possibilities and move into action.
- **Encourager**: I am at my best when I believe in others and challenge them to step out in faith.

The result? These five words become a first look at your role and how you deliver your influence to others. Opportunities that allow for the expression of these five words should be given serious consideration.

Here is an example of one individual's Five Words woven together into a descriptive statement:

Five Words: Catalyze, empower, challenge, generosity, vulnerability

Descriptive statement: I seek to catalyze and empower leaders who are called by God to launch new expressions of the church, by offering my resources and access to my life.

FIVE CIRCLES

The life of Jesus reflects a series of relationships that can be seen in concentric circles. Each circle was a group of people or individuals with whom Jesus had relationship and into which He invested time and training. The closer to the center, the greater the time and level of intimacy. The more outward the circles, the more Jesus cultivated interest in following Him. The concentric circles moved from Peter (the centermost circle), to Peter, James, John, to the disciples, to the fifty to the 120.

It's not so much the number of people that matters, but rather, the various ways and levels of influencing and investing in others.

This construct provides a template for identifying those you can or need to influence in the days ahead.

As you think about your future, who could be your "Peter?"

Who could be your "Peter, James and John?"

Who could be your smaller group of 6-12?

What could be your larger church/organization that you may be called to influence?

What could be your wider Kingdom influence?

By becoming intentional, you create a greater potential for influence and impact. Note that Jesus used various means and methods with each group. Take a piece of paper and draw out the five concentric circles. Begin to brainstorm and name who could fit within each circle. Use the previous exercise (Five Words) to think about those who would value your contribution the most.

The result? This Five Circles exercise helps to combine what you offer with whom you could offer it to in the future.

THIRTEEN WAYS

Leaving behind a legacy requires clarity of one's ultimate contribution. As a Christ-follower ages, he/she gains clarity in how God has shaped their life, and what they should focus on during their remaining years.

Clarifying one's ultimate contribution type can help those who are committed to finishing well think productively and continue to contribute at the end. Younger believers who begin to think this way can more proactively move toward a better defined legacy much earlier in their life and ministry.

An ultimate contribution is a Christ-follower's lasting legacy for which he or she is remembered and which furthers the cause of Christ's Kingdom. Characteristics of ultimate contribution often are made up of one or more of the following:

- Values and convictions related to life and ministry
- Impacting others by new approaches and innovation
- Serving as a stimulus for change which advances the Church and impacts the world
- Leaving behind an organization, institution, or movement that will further God's Kingdom work

three constructs

- The discovery of ideas, concepts and methods of communication that serve to advance the current thinking and/or paradigms

The research of Dr. J. Robert Clinton, included in his book *Focused Lives*, surfaced thirteen types of ultimate contribution. These include:

1. Model—One who lives a godly life, who is always seeking to go deeper with God, and lives a life that others want to emulate
2. Practitioner—One who lives life in such a way that sets the pace for others and invites others to follow.
3. Family—One who promotes a God-fearing family that produces children who walk with God and carry on a Godly heritage.
4. Mentor/Coach—One who serves others by offering support and empowering individuals and groups, etc.
5. Communicator—One who possesses an ability to speak and communicate with large groups.
6. Pioneer—One who brings something new into existence.
7. Change Agent—One who instigates change, helps right the wrongs and goes after injustices in our society and in the Church
8. Artist—One who has creative expression of thoughts and/or ideas and brings breakthroughs in life and ministry
9. Founder—One who starts new organizations or ministries that meet needs or capture new expressions of life
10. Stabilizer—One who often offers strength by organizing and involving others, helping them to develop greater stability.
11. Researcher—One who gleans new ideation and insights through in-depth study of various topics.
12. Writer—One who captures ideas and reproduces them in written format

13. Promoter—One who effectively distributes new ideas, methods and/or approaches

Most of us are a combination of these types. A useful way to illustrate one's unique and ultimate contribution is to place a combination of these 13 types within a series of concentric circles.

Concentric Circle Exercise

First, choose 3 types that best describe you. Next, arrange them in the concentric circles with the type that *most* describes who you are and your influence on others, in the center circle.

Example

In the center: *Writer*
In the mid-ring: *Promoter*
On the outside: *Change agent*

These three types could be woven together into a statement that points to this Christ-follower's ultimate contribution, such as:

I write and develop resources that serve to be a catalyst for change among Christian leaders.

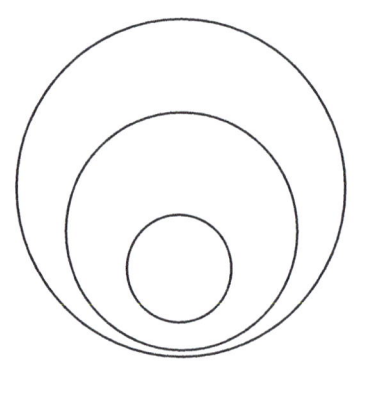

Convergence brings together who you are and what God has shaped you to do. The example statement above is not complete, but provides a place to begin as an individual starts to spell out their contribution to others, and the unique influence that they can pass on to others. You cannot pass on what you don't know that you have. The articulation of one's contribution type provides a beginning point for understanding what you have to give to others.

WANT MORE?

Here is a link to Leader Breakthru's website that will take you further on topics covered in this chapter:

www.leaderbreakthru.com/convergence

15
the value of coaching

*The purposes of a person's heart are deep waters,
but one who has insight draws them out.*
— PROVERBS 20:5

*Coaching is about learning to coach the person,
instead of just the problem.*
— TERRY WALLING

It is often a difficult task to determine what you have to offer others at the end-game, and harder still discerning who to invest in and share what God has entrusted to you. The insights shared thus far have been attempts to bridge both of those challenges. *Resonance*, an online, personal discovery process from Leader Breakthru, builds on many of the insights in this book, and continues your discernment process. You can purchase access to the *Resonance Online Process* by visiting, www.leaderbreakthru.com/resonance. The process consists of eight online sessions and a downloadable workbook, and takes approximate 6-8 hours to complete. It is a step-by-step, guided time of reflection and application that helps you to further distill your insights by:

- Defining your contribution to others
- Identifying obstacles to finishing well
- Recognizing who God has positioned you to help
- Understanding the power of coming alongside
- Creating a Personal Legacy Statement

Each of these resources help to advance your approach to this critical stage in your development, but we do not get to clarity alone. You need a coach.

COACHING

Coaching is different than you might the think. The role of a coach is to draw out insights that are within you, but as of yet have not been voiced. Mentors walk before and deposit insights within. Typically, those facing the Finishing Transition will need both—a coach who will draw out insights, and periodic mentoring that can provide additional clarity. While all of us benefit from mentoring, the greatest need for those in the Finishing Transition is often coaching.

The benefits of coaching can be summed up in one word: **perspective**. Most people who face this transition are submerged in the situation, and are unable to see God's sovereign purpose. By asking discovery-based questions, coaches help those experiencing transitions to be better able to recognize God's shaping work.

The role of a coach is threefold:

1. To help encourage and *recognize* the greater work God desires to do
2. To help an individual *process* what God is doing
3. To help an individual *consider* the choices they face in light of God's work

One of the most important contributions a coach can make for those experiencing the Finishing Transition is to challenge one's thinking with regards to role and future influence. Many who face this transition struggle to see the future, and what their role should now be. Identifying restricting paradigms or beliefs is something that (often) only a trusted coach can do.

The posture of a coach is to walk with an individual during strategic moments of their journey with Christ—helping one to recognize God's voice. Too much of life has already passed, and the days ahead are too important to not consider securing the help of a coach.

Coaches walk beside and help draw insights out.

Mentors go before and help place insights within.

All of us need both as we travel through life.

Coaches are invaluable at the end-game.

At stake is the ability to finish well.

Here are a few additional thoughts.

1. **We don't get to clarity alone.** In Proverbs 27:17 we see this truth, *"As iron sharpens iron, so a friend sharpens a friend."* We need other people in our lives to sharpen us and to be a sounding board for what God is doing in us.

2. **What we discover, we own.** Christ-followers who navigate times of transition need to own the conclusions they come to in order to take responsibility for the changes that will be required. Coaches promote discovery. Most of us resist what we are told, but we embrace what we discover. A coach's role is not to tell or teach, but to ask, listen and facilitate a process of discovery—helping others to "mine the gold" from within.

3. **Listening is about hearing what is said, and what is not said.** A good coach will be listening to words as well as to the insights and feelings between the words. It is important to go beneath the surface and help people process what's behind the words.

4. **Asking questions begins the process of change.** As soon as the first question is asked, the change begins. Open-ended questions that promote greater reflection and self-discovery are critical. Coaches can also help you listen not only to yourselves but to what the Spirit of God is highlighting. Coaches are critical.

THE IDEA COACHING PATHWAY

Having a path for a structured coaching conversation can make the difference between a helpful talk and a breakthrough. The *IDEA Coaching Pathway*[19] offers four stepping-stones that serve to guide an effective coaching conversation. The four steps of IDEA are: Identify, Discover, Evaluate and Act.

Identify: The first step is to connect with the person and begin to build rapport and trust. We coach the person, not just the problem. It's important to identify the core desire and outcome that should be achieved from the conversation.

Discover: The second step down the path of clarity is to explore the issues and circumstances related to one's core desire/outcome. They will present through questions and active listening.

Evaluate: The third step is to discern how God might be working through this situation, issue, or problem to shape the person, and to pinpoint the issue that is holding one back from the desired solution.

Act: The final step down the *IDEA Coaching Pathway* is to help the individual being coached to develop 1-2 strategic, S.M.A.R.T. actions steps, and then to close the conversation by reviewing their take-away.

FINDING A COACH

Looking for someone to coach you as you walk through the Finishing Transition? Find a coach at www.leaderbreakthru.com/coaching.

A FINAL NOTE

As this book comes to its close, it also brings to a close our book series that chronicles the three defining moments in the life of a Christ-follower—the Awakening Transition, the Deciding Transition, and now the Finishing Transition. In my book *Stuck!* I compare the journey through these three transition moments to the death-defying act that is performed by trapeze artists at a circus.[37]

The Awakening Transition occurs at the beginning of one's journey, and is like those first moments of the trapeze act, as a flyer climbs up the high rope ladder to the small platform above and makes the difficult and risky decision to jump.

The Deciding Transition is similar to that moment when the flyer's rhythmic back and forth motion has generated enough momentum that they leave the safety of their swing and fly toward the catcher—suspended on a swing and eagerly awaiting the arrival of the flyer. At some point in our life we must let go—we must make choices to be who God made us to be. As we do, the strong hands of our Catcher reward our trust with a secure grasp, and then provide us with a new momentum that is greater than we could ever achieve alone.

The Finishing Transition is about that arrival home—back to the platform where the other flyers are awaiting our return. But before we can return to the platform, we must experience that final release from the catcher, that final grasp of the swing, and that final push to the platform—to home. As we have discussed in this book, the Finishing Transition launches the completion of the journey and the legacy of a life that has sought to finish well, and hear the words *"well done."*

When I wrote *Stuck!* I was facing the Deciding Transition. I have now experienced the Finishing Transition and I am heading home. I am not finished, but I have recaptured that swing and my movement back to the platform has begun. Little did I know that writing these four books about transitions, and coaching passionate Christ-followers like yourself through these defining moments would be part of my legacy. But that is how the journey goes. Transitions help to take us to new places. Sometimes these places are different than the ones we had planned, or had thought were on our horizon. But these places are known to our creator God. Our task is to discover how God is at work, and to join Him in that work, even when it is hard to see. His role is to continue to lead us to the *"good works, which God prepared in advance for us to do."* (Ephesians 2:10)

> *"Being confident of this, that he who began a good work in you will carry it on to completion until the day of Christ Jesus."*
> —Philipians 1:6

notes

[1] Sara Lawrence-Lightfoot, *The Third Chapter*, (Sara Crichton Books, 2009), p. 29

[2] Lawrence-Lightfoot, p. 121

[3] C.S. Lewis, as quoted by Good Reads

[4] Jim Elliott, from his personal journal entry, Oct. 28, 1949)

[5] C.S. Lewis, *Joyful Christian*, (Simon and Schuster, 1996), p.180

[6] David Platt, *A Compassionate Call to Counter Culture in a World of Poverty, Same-Sex Marriage, Racism, Sex Slavery, Immigration, Abortion, Persecution, Orphans and Pornography,* (Tyndale House Publishers, Inc., 2016)

[7] J.I. Packer, http://christian-quotes.ochristian.com/J.I.-Packer-Quotes

[8] Sara Lawrence-Lightfoot, p. 40

[9] Sara Lawrence-Lightfoot, p. 52

[10] Sara Lawrence-Lightfoot, p. 56

[11] Experience Corps, *Fact Sheet on Aging America*. Washington, DC, 2000

[12] AARP 2012 Study: *Staying Ahead of the Curve*

[13] U.S Census Bureau, 2005

[14] John Piper, Desiring God Video

[15] Francis Chan, *Crazy Love: Overwhelmed by a Relentless God,* (David C. Cook, 2015)

[16] Randy Alcorn, *The Treasure Principle: Discovering the Secret of Joyful Giving,* (Multnomah, 2012), p. 49

[17] Henry Ward Beecher Quotes. (n.d.). BrainyQuote.com. Retrieved September 3, 2019, from BrainyQuote.com Web site: https://www.brainyquote.com/quotes/henry_ward_beecher_150037

[18] David Brenner, *The Gift of Being Yourself: The Sacred Call to Self-Discovery,* (IVP Books; Expanded edition, 2015)

[19] Terry Walling, *IDEA Coaching Pathway,* www.leaderbreakthru.com/idea

[20] David Platt, *Radical: Taking Back Your Faith from the American Dream,* (Multnomah, 2010)

[21] Oswald Chambers, *My Utmost for His Highest,* (Discovery House; Revised edition, 1992)

[22] Alan Redpath. (n.d.). AZQuotes.com. Retrieved September 03, 2019, from AZQuotes.com Web site: https://www.azquotes.com/quote/815906

[23] Richard J. Foster, *Richard Foster's treasury of Christian discipline,* (Jossey-Bass, 1995*)

[24] Corrie Ten Boom, as quoted by Good Reads

[25] Leader Breakthru Inc., *Coach Certificate Training,* www.leaderbrekathru.com/coach-certificate

[26] Ravi Zacharias, *I, Isaac, Take Thee, Rebekah: Moving from Romance to Lasting Love,* (Thomas Nelson Inc, 2005), p. 25

[27] Henri J. Nouwen, as quoted by Good Reads

[28] Eugene Peterson, *The Jesus Way: A Conversation on the Ways That Jesus Is the Way,* (Eerdmans; Reprint edition, 2011)

[29] Chuck Swindoll, *Three Steps Forwards, Two Steps Back,* (Thomas Nelson Inc., 1997) p. 34

[30] C.S. Lewis, *Personal Quotes/Biography,* imdb.com

[31] Dick Lucas, as quoted by Timothy Keller, *Every Good Endeavor,* (Penguin Books; Reprint edition, 2014), p. 119

[32] Watchman Nee, *Journeying Towards the Spiritual: A Digest of the Spiritual Man in 42 Lessons",* (Chrisitan Fellowship Publishers, 2006), p. 161

[33] J. I. Packer. (n.d.). AZQuotes.com. Retrieved September 03, 2019, from AZQuotes.com Web site: https://www.azquotes.com/quote/532815

[34] C.S. Lewis, *Joyful Christian,* (Simon and Schuster, 1996), p.180

35. Dwight L. Moody. (n.d.). AZQuotes.com. Retrieved September 03, 2019, from AZQuotes.com Web site: https://www.azquotes.com/quote/540420

36. Martin Luther. (n.d.). AZQuotes.com. Retrieved September 03, 2019, from AZQuotes.com Web site: https://www.azquotes.com/quote/180785

37. Terry Walling, *Stuck! Navigating the Transitions of Life & Leadership*, CreateSpace Independent Publishing Platform; Revised edition, 2015), p. 76-78

Appendix A.
Small Group Guide

A RESOURCE FOR SMALL GROUPS, READING GROUPS OR PEER COACHING GROUPS

This resource is meant to guide a small group, book club or peer coaching group through *Finishing*. The following pages provide a week-by-week outline to facilitate small group discussion. It has been designed so that the facilitation of the meeting can be shared. A basic script is provided in italics for the facilitator and discussion questions are included for each weekly meeting.

TYPICAL SMALL GROUP FORMAT

Week One:

Introduce the book and hear each person's personal story.

For Next Time—Assignment: Read chapters 1-3

Week Two:

Discuss chapters 1-3 / Share Insights about the Finishing Transition

For Next Time—Assignment: Read chapters 4-5

Week Three:

Discuss chapters 4-5 / Entry and Evaluation

For Next Time—Assignment: Read chapters 6-7

Week Four:

Discuss chapters 6-7 / Alignment and Direction

For Next Time—Assignment: Read chapter 8

Week Five:

Discuss chapter 8 / Resolve and Challenges

For Next Time—Assignment: Read chapters 9-12

Week Six:

Discuss chapters 9-12 / The Applications

For Next Time—Assignment: Read chapters 13-15

Week Seven:

Discuss chapters 13-15 / The Helps

For Next Time—Assignment: Summarize your insights from the book

Week Eight:

Summary Discussions / Share insights / Next steps regarding the Finishing Transition

WEEK ONE—INTRODUCTION & STORIES

> "Each of us will go through a series of transitions as we journey with Christ. The question is not whether we will go through transitions, but rather, have our transitions gone through us, and have we gained all we can out of them."

> "For the next eight weeks, we will be going through the book Finishing together and will be discussing topics around the Finishing Transition. Finishing is divided into four parts: The Purpose, The Bridge, The Applications and The Helps. We will be reading chapters in advance of our meeting and then discussing the reading material together. We will share our thoughts and will also be guided through some discussion questions that are included in this guide."

Have someone volunteer to read the section Getting the Most Out of Finishing on pages 12 and 13.

> "How do you each of you currently view your journey with Christ in light of the issues presented in this passage and the overview of the book."

Personal Stories

> "We're going to spend the rest of our time together sharing our stories with the rest of the group. Each person will introduce themselves and then will reflect on and answer these three questions."

- "What are you hoping to gain through this reading/discussion?"
- "How would you describe your current situation?"
- "Do you currently feel you are in a time of transition?

> "I (the facilitator) will go first."

> "Let's close our time together by praying and asking the Spirit of God to lead and guide our discussion and learning during our weeks together."

Assignment: *Read chapters 1-3*

WEEK TWO—ESSENTIALS OF THE FINISHING TRANSITION

"The purpose of this time is to review some of the core foundations of the book related to the concept of transitions in general and of the Finishing Transition specifically. Let's open with a time of prayer."

Discussion Questions

Use the following questions to help the group to discuss the contents of chapters 1-3.

- *"Share 1-2 overall highlights from the three chapters. What stood out to you?"*

- *"How could you know that God is moving someone into a time of transition and potentially Convergence? From chapter one, what are some thoughts about transitions, how they occur and how to recognize if you are in one? Who feels that they may be experiencing a time of transition? What are some of your current struggles, challenges or questions?"*

- *"From chapter two, review the cultural norms on pages 34-36. Discuss how each norm could potentially affect your view of the end-game and run counter to the purpose of God's shaping. Which of the norms do you feel may be having the greatest impact on you in this season?"*

- *"This next set of questions has to do with the topic of Convergence."*
    - *"How does the author describe the season of Convergence?"*
    - *"What do you see as the essentials of Convergence?"*

- *"Is there anything else that stands out, or questions these insights might have raised?"*

Allow the group to discuss other thoughts that surfaced from the first three chapters.

"Let's close our time together in prayer."

Assignment: *Read chapters 4-5 (Note that chapters of 4-8 are written in narrative form, highlighting the Finishing Transition of Robert Grant).*

WEEK THREE—ENTRY & EVALUATION

Open the meeting with a time to reconnect and pray.

> "Let's begin by turning to page 24 to review the Transition Life Cycle. The Transition Life Cycle depicts a generic path that a transition often takes."

> "Note that each of the next four chapters correspond to the Lifecycle segments: Entry, Evaluation, Alignment, and Direction. This week's meeting seeks to highlight the Entry and Evaluation phases of the Finishing Transition."

Discussion Questions

- "Share 1-2 overall highlights from chapters 4 and 5. What stood out from the reading and the concepts?"

- "In chapter four, the coaching conversation depicts Robert as he surfaces the idea of being set aside during a time when real contribution is desired. What stood out to you related to how the transition began? What was Robert experiencing? What did you draw from Robert's need to step back from the situation and gain perspective?"

- Let's review Robert's reflections on page 57 and then let's discuss the issue of one's identity being tied to one's work or position"

- "Let's talk about how this could be impacting us. What have you seen in others whose identity is built around their work? What is their greatest struggle? What (if any) could your struggle be?"

- Chapter five talked about key turning points in Robert's journey, and the lessons and patterns he was able to recognize in terms of God's shaping work in his life. Ask participants to share ONE significant moment from their journey and how God used that experience to direct their lives and shape their contribution to others.

Closure Questions

- "What might our past be telling us about how God wants to use us in the future?"
- "What was most helpful or what was most insightful from these chapters and our discussion of the first two phases of the Finishing Transition?"

"Let's close our time together in prayer"

Assignment: *Read chapters 6-7 and be prepared to discuss them at our next time together.*

WEEK FOUR—ALIGNMENT & DIRECTION

Open the meeting with a time to reconnect and pray.

"Before we head into our discussion, let's share any way we have been able to use the concepts thus far, or any way that we are processing where we are in our journey?"

"If you feel you may be experiencing the Finishing Transition, have you received additional clarity or insight related to what's next or where God might be leading?"

Allow time for open dialog and interaction.

"In our time together we will now focus on the second-half of the Finishing Transition; the Alignment and Direction segments."

Discussion Questions

- "Share 1-2 overall highlights from chapters 6 and 7. What stood out to you from reading about these two phases?"
- "Let's focus our discussion first on the issue of Alignment."
    - "Would anyone like to comment on what Robert shared about the pattern of hurt he identified in his journey? What could be the value of the Closure Paper?"
    - "How could one's wounding in the past impact one's ability to finish well and be able to navigate this stage of the journey?"

- "In chapter seven, God begins to use the transition to reveal both purpose and direction to Robert. Talk about how direction was beginning to come for Robert, and other ways God might begin to provide direction and the way forward."
- "Review pages 88 and 89, and the issues related to his Finishing Transition. Talk about what the keys were to Robert beginning to see purpose and new light."

"The focus of this discussion was to see how God can bring direction as a result of the Finishing Transition. Some of us may feel like we need direction right now, but we have not been able to breakthrough. Let's spend some time praying for those of us who feel we are experiencing a time of transition. Let's pray for the ability to begin to see new direction and answers in the days ahead."

"Let's close our time together in prayer"

Assignment: *Read chapter 8.*

WEEK FIVE—RESOLVE & CHALLENGES

Open the meeting with a time to reconnect and pray.

"This time, our discussion focuses on the ending of Robert's narrative through his Finishing Transition. Our focus is on how God calls us into Convergence and with it, greater faith and trust."

"It is a good time to look back and review together what we've learned about this transition that moves us from discovering our calling to clarifying our unique, Kingdom contribution."

"Let's spend a little bit of time going back and remembering how the Finishing Transition occurs and the ways God uses this time to shape our lives. First, let's review the Transition Life Cycle:"

Entry: *What do we remember about what launches someone into this transition?*

Evaluation: What surfaced in the work God began to do during this transition?

Alignment: How does God pinpoint issues we need to address to move forward?

Direction: How do we begin to recognize when the transition is coming to an end?

"Now, let's think back and review some of the ways God works during a transition and how He often surfaces issues related to those paradigms or obstacles that could hold back our development."

"For the remainder of our time, let's shift our attention to chapter 8 and to the resolve required to keep moving, and to move beyond the time of transition."

Discussion Questions

- "Share 1-2 overall highlights from chapter 8. What stood out to you about Faith Challenge?"
- "How do you feel about some of the choices that often need to be made as a result of a transition? What were some of Robert's choices that lay ahead of him? What are some of the choices that could await you?"
- "Determining future direction and Faith Challenges will often take time and will require a resolve to step beyond one's current circumstances. What could be some of your greatest challenges?"

Ask the participants to summarize the discussion from the group.

"Let's close our time together in prayer."

Assignment: Read chapters 9-12

WEEK SIX—THE APPLICATIONS

Open the meeting with a time to reconnect and pray.

"In our time of discussion this week, we get the chance to process how the issues in the Finishing Transition often impact each of us *differently, depending on who we are and the contexts that we find ourselves in."*

Discussion Questions

- *"Share 1-2 overall highlights from chapters 9 and 10 and how both men and women might process the Finishing Transition."*
- *"Share 1-2 insights from chapters 11 and 12 and how one's life stage impacts how to navigate the transition better?"*
- *"Let's discuss how women and men could process the Finishing Transition in a similar way or in a different way. Review pages 95-99 and the three practices related to both men and women. What was helpful? How are you processing the transition?"*
- *"Let's contrast the three contexts discussed in chapter 10: Ministry, Marketplace and the Home. What does the context do to the ways God works during this period of time? What is unique to each setting and what is similar?"*
- *"Now let's move the discussion to those who are encountering the Finishing Transition before ending full-time employment, and those who're experiencing the transition after ending full-time employment."*
  - *"Those who experience the transition before (pre) are often facing questions of needing to sort through what is actually occurring, and what it could mean in the days ahead. Review and discuss the What-How-Why diagram on page 112 and use this time to clarify all three questions."*
  - *"Those who experience the transition following (post) retirement are often facing questions about needing to sort current activities and deciding what to engage in. Discuss the Four Questions exercise and their value to helping sort through how to move forward."*
- *"Let's pair up and share what these discussions have been revealing to us, Then, let's pray for each other to be able to hear God's voice and overcome the obstacles we each might be facing."*

Assignment: *Read chapters 13-15*

WEEK SEVEN—THE HELPS

> *"Since we are almost finished with our work through* Finishing, *let's spend a few minutes sharing ideas about how we may want to wrap up our time together (i.e., dinner together, dessert, talking about a next book, etc.)"*

Allow the group to discuss. Decide together what (if any) should be the group's plan for the next time. Open the meeting with a time to reconnect and pray.

> *"Our reading this week focused on more practical issues that often surround the Finishing Transition. Sometimes people can feel they need to process their times of transition on their own. But a proper understanding of our need for community moves us past issues of independence, or dependence, and onto becoming healthy individuals who seek interdependent relationships and the feedback from those who know our hearts."*

> *"Tonight we will review the various helps offered in chapters 13-15 and how each can help us process the ongoing work of the Finishing Transition."*

Discussion Questions

- *"Let's review the Four Postures and their definitions on page 125. The Four Postures exercise highlights four mindsets that help foster the environment of Convergence and make one's life accessible to those they can potentially influence. Which is most applicable to you? What do you feel should be your focus?"*

- *"The Three Constructs and Five Words exercises were designed to surface a first draft of a Christ-follower's unique contribution. What helped? What is still confusing? What needs more work or the help of others?"*

- *"The Thirteen Ways reflect unique types and combinations of influence that those who finish well often display. The combining of a few of these types helps one define what their unique role could be during their time of Convergence. Let's review the thirteen types and discuss how they apply to the each of us."*

- "Let's break into groups of 3-4 and talk further about which of the constructs is most applicable to our personal situations."

Allow for the informal time of interaction and discussion.

Note the coaching process that is discussed in chapter 15. The *Resonance Process* and coaching are for those who want to go deeper in understanding and clarifying their unique contribution. (www.leaderbreakthru.com/resonance)

> **Closing:** *"Let's close our time by sharing one insight about how we will continue to process our time of transition."*
>
> *"Next week we will focus on summarizing our insights from the book, and its application to each of our journeys with Christ. "*
>
> *"Between now and our next time together, look back through the book at the things you highlighted from your reading. Bring 2-3 insights you want to take with you into the future."*
>
> *"Let's close our time together in prayer."*

WEEK EIGHT—SUMMARIZING INSIGHTS

Groups often use a meal or dessert time to close their discussion of a book like *Finishing*.

After some informal time together, go around and ask each member to share what stood out to them.

> *"Let's go around the room and share the 2-3 big insights that we are taking away from our time going through this book."*

Note: If the group wants to continue digging into this topic together, introduce the idea of working through the *Resonance Online Process* as a group. Each person registers for the online process, and Leader Breakthru offers a Small Group Discussion Guide. Visit www.leaderbreakthru.com/resonance for more information

> *"Let's close our time together in prayer, thanking God for the discussion and insights that have been gained."*

Appendix B.
Coach's Guide & Questions

COACHING THE FINISHING TRANSITION USING THIS BOOK

Issue: Moving Into Convergence

Topics: Influence

Typical Coaching Series: Six Coaching Appointments / 45 min. each

SESSION 1:
Overview Convergence and a time of transition
Read chapters 1-3

SESSION 2:
Overview the coachee's past turning points and insights (review Post-It Note Timeline, if created)
Read chapters 4-5

SESSION 3:
Discuss issues God is surfacing.
Read chapters 6-7

SESSION 4:
Discuss issues of alignment and the first run at Convergence
Read chapters 8-9

SESSION 5:
Refine Contribution and Convergence
Read chapters 10-12

SESSION 6:
Discuss obstacles and challenges as the individual moves beyond the Finishing Transition.
Read chapters 13-15

COACHING QUESTIONS: CONTRIBUTION

- If I were to ask someone who knows you well, what would they say is the way you have influenced their life the most?

- Talk about the few things you would love to do more of, or focus on, if you just had more time.

- What do you find yourself saying "yes" to more than you should? What are you not saying "no" to that you know you should?

- How has God worked in the past when you faced a moment that is similar? What, typically, are some of the things He does to help give you direction? Assurance?

- When others have affirmed that God has used you in their life, what do they say? What are they typically telling you that you do well?

- What choices do you know you need to make in the days ahead to be able to do more of what God has shaped you to do?

- What major roadblocks need to be overcome in order for you to be free to be you in the days ahead?

- What do you have to offer?

- How would you describe your influence to others?

- How does your current work/job let you live out this influence?

- Of all that you do, when do you feel you are most being you?

- What part of your job allows you to live into being you?

- What parts of your job keep you from being you?

- What might need to be enhanced in your job? Adjusted? Changed?

- How do you currently make important decisions?

- How do your core methods help you live out your role?

- What are the interior issues God seems to be addressing? Readdressing?

TRANSITION QUESTIONS: PROCESSING GOD'S SHAPING WORK

The processing of a transition often brings up issues and insights God is seeking to bring to the surface during this "in-between" moment of the journey. Here are issues that often occur, and processing questions as you look at your own journey, or that of another.

Isolation: *When a leader is set aside from normal influence/involvement to hear from God.*

- What are you sensing about being connected to the people or events around you?
- What does God seem to be saying/doing when you're alone?

Life Crisis: *When a leader experiences special intense situations of pressure in human experiences that test and teach dependence.*

- Talk to me about the impact of all these recent events on you and your view of things.
- Where (or to whom) do you often go when these types of things happen to you?

Leadership Backlash: *When a leader experiences conflicts in ministry, work, or on a team and gets resistance from followers.*

- As hard as it is to experience people's rejection and hurt, what could this be teaching you about how God can use these moments to forge character?
- What are you sensing it is doing to you and your values or convictions?

Negative Preparation: *When a leader experiences difficult circumstances that dislodge and free them to move on to their next stage of development.*

- How are all of these experiences impacting your overall development as a leader?

- Are their people in your life who have a "big picture" view of your situation? What are they telling you?

Integrity Checks: *A test that God uses to evaluate whether a leader's heart and inner convictions are consistent with their outward actions.*

- Tell me what you think is being tested inside of you right now.
- If you could state in one or two words the core conviction this is touching within you, what would they be?

Obedience Checks: *A test of a leader's capacity to hear from God and to respond through intentional steps or actions in order to align with God's purposes.*

- Tell me about new ways that God is calling you to trust Him.
- What's the core action or behavior you believe God is asking you to take?

Word Checks: *A test of a leader's capacity to hear from God and from His Word and to apply revelation to their life and ministry.*

- Tell me what's coming to you out of the Word right now as you reflect on this.
- What's the core action or behavior you believe God is asking you to take?

Divine Contact: *When a leader comes in contact with a key person at a crucial moment that helps ensure future development.*

- Who are the people God uses to speak into your life? Trusted friend? Out of the blue?
- How do they typically get through to you?
- Who has God used the most to speak into your life? What are they saying to you about this situation?

Destiny Experiences: *When a leader hears God speaking/intervening with insight concerning future direction and destiny.*

- Tell me about what you sense God was doing/saying by allowing this to happen.
- How does your experience right now line up with the last several months?

Destiny Revelation: *A test of a leader's capacity to hear from God concerning future direction and ultimate destiny.*

- What or how did you realize this was God actually speaking or "connecting the dots?"
- Has this same truth been confirmed in other ways to you?

Destiny Fulfillment: *Moments when God's direction and desires come into existence and the next steps are made clear.*

- Look back and talk to me about how this fits in to your overall life/development.
- Tell me how you see all these things fitting together. What makes it more than just circumstantial?

Faith Challenge: *A test of a leader's willingness to take steps of faith and grow in capacity to trust God.*

- How did you realize that this was God actually speaking to you to step out?
- Has this same truth been confirmed in other ways to you?

Appendix C
Closure Paper Template

The purpose of this 1-2 page summary is to bring closure to a chapter in one's development—an important experience, assignment or vocational role—in order to better move into the future and into all that God has for you. Often we do not gain closure from what we have experienced, which leaves lessons on the table and increases the potential of repeating past struggles. Here is a five-part template for writing a Closure Paper.

PART 1:

What are the key lessons you learned from this past experience? List these in bullet form with each lesson no more than two sentences. The fewer the words, the greater the access into the future.
Example: You do not get to clarity alone.

PART 2:

In what way did God use this experience to develop you as a person, and develop your character? Summarize your thoughts.
Example: I was able to recognize that my value comes from who I am, as opposed to what I do. I will always be re-learning this truth.

PART 3:

In what way did God use this experience to reveal your abilities, skills and contribution you make to others?
Example: I now recognize that my greatest influence comes from being alongside others and coaching their growth and development.

PART 4:

What did you learn about you, your God and His purposes? How did He use the difficult moments of this experience to shape you, and what do you need to continue to work through as a result of this experience?
Example: I realize that I seek the approval of others to the point that it can cloud my judgement and can cause me to not finish well.

PART 5:

What are the 2-3 most important lessons you learned from this period of time that you want to make sure you remember, and take with you in the days ahead?

Examples:

- *People are my most important ministry.*
- *Being me is my greatest act of worship*

the leadership development series

Leader Brekathru's Leadership Development Series consists of three books that take a closer look at the three significant transition moments that every Christ-follower will face. Each of these books can be used as a personal read, a small group resource or as a one-on-one coaching resource. For an introduction to the concept of transitions and an overview of these transitions, check out the book *Stuck! Navigating the Transitions of Life & Leadership*, by Terry Walling.

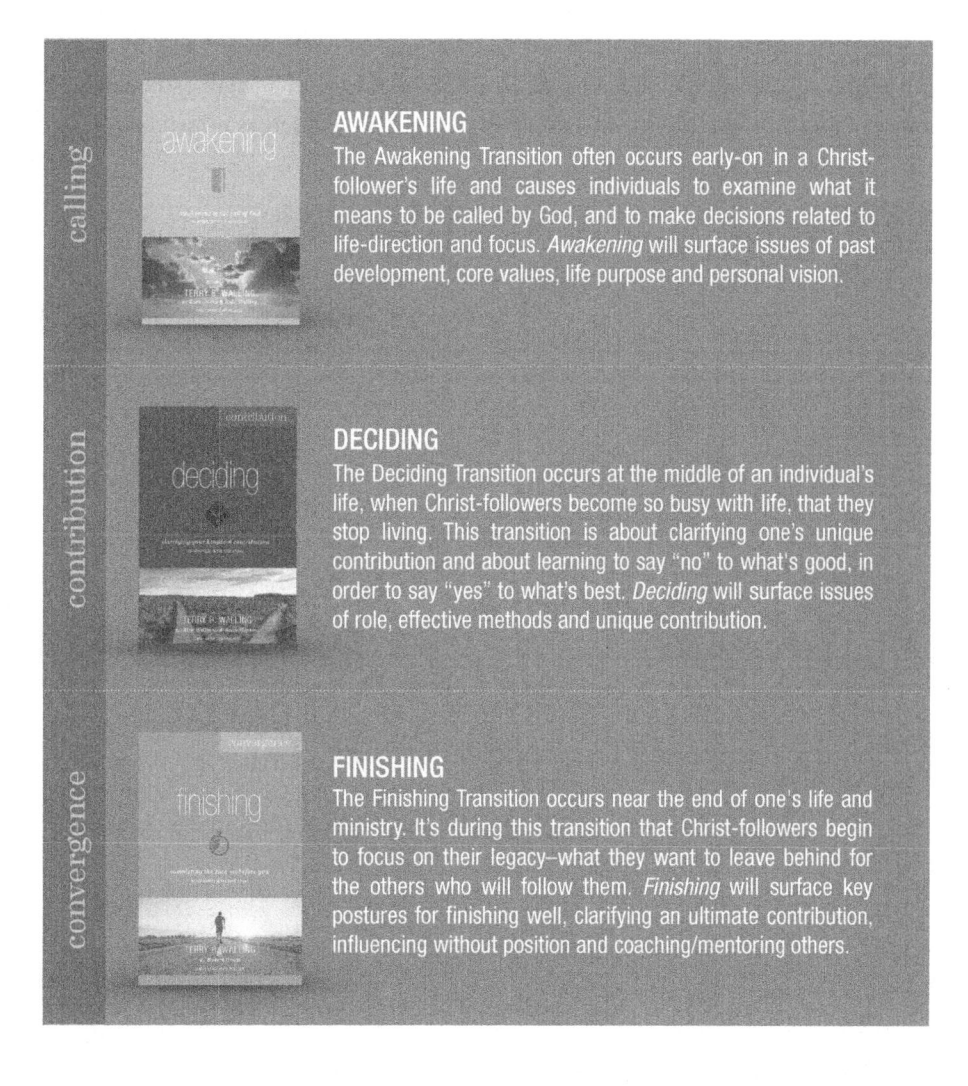

AWAKENING
The Awakening Transition often occurs early-on in a Christ-follower's life and causes individuals to examine what it means to be called by God, and to make decisions related to life-direction and focus. *Awakening* will surface issues of past development, core values, life purpose and personal vision.

DECIDING
The Deciding Transition occurs at the middle of an individual's life, when Christ-followers become so busy with life, that they stop living. This transition is about clarifying one's unique contribution and about learning to say "no" to what's good, in order to say "yes" to what's best. *Deciding* will surface issues of role, effective methods and unique contribution.

FINISHING
The Finishing Transition occurs near the end of one's life and ministry. It's during this transition that Christ-followers begin to focus on their legacy—what they want to leave behind for the others who will follow them. *Finishing* will surface key postures for finishing well, clarifying an ultimate contribution, influencing without position and coaching/mentoring others.

3 Core Processes™

Leader Breakthru offers three core, personal development processes that are designed to guide the on-going development of a Christ-follower. Together they comprise a leadership development system for churches, missions, ministries and organizations.

If you'd like more information about these processes, would like to go through one of the processes online, or would like to gain a license to facilitate one of the processes in your context, please visit: leaderbreakthru.com

FOCUSED LIVING
The Focused Living Process consists of six-sessions related to clarifying life direction and personal calling. This process helps leaders and all Christ-followers gain perspective through the development of core values, a statement of being (life purpose) and a statement of doing (personal vision).

APEX
The APEX Process consists of eight-sessions that bring greater clarity to a Christ-follower's unique, personal contribution. This process will help individuals discover issues related to their major role and effective methods, and will provide a decision-making grid called a "Personal Life Mandate" that will help to guide any choices that lay ahead.

RESONANCE
The Resonance Process is a series of three preparatory meetings and three strategic discussions by those who love Christ and desire to finish well. This process helps Christ-followers to clarify how to have influence without position, empower others and leave behind a godly legacy.

Made in the
USA
Monee, IL